IN THE WARS
OF THE ROSES

A Story for the Young

EVERETT EVELYN-GREEN

1st WORLD
LIBRARY
Literary Society

In the Wars of the Roses

Evelyn Everett-Green

© 1st World Library, 2007
PO Box 2211
Fairfield, IA 52556
www.1stworldlibrary.com
First Edition

LCCN: 2007930781

Softcover ISBN: 978-1-4218-4819-8
Hardcover ISBN: 978-1-4218-4722-1
eBook ISBN: 978-1-4218-4916-4

Purchase *"In the Wars of the Roses"*
as a traditional bound book at:
www.1stWorldLibrary.com/purchase.asp?ISBN=978-1-4218-4819-8

1st World Library is a literary, educational organization
dedicated to:

- Creating a free internet library of downloadable ebooks

- Hosting writing competitions and offering book publishing
  scholarships.

Interested in more 1st World Library books? contact:
literacy@1stworldlibrary.com
Check us out at: www.1stworldlibrary.com

1st World Library Literary Society

Giving Back to the World

"If you want to work on the core problem, it's early school literacy."

- **James Barksdale, former CEO of Netscape**

"No skill is more crucial to the future of a child, or to a democratic and prosperous society, than literacy."

- **Los Angeles Times**

"Literacy... means far more than learning how to read and write... The aim is to transmit... knowledge and promote social participation."

- **UNESCO**

"Literacy is not a luxury, it is a right and a responsibility. If our world is to meet the challenges of the twenty-first century we must harness the energy and creativity of all our citizens."

- **President Bill Clinton**

"Parents should be encouraged to read to their children, and teachers should be equipped with all available techniques for teaching literacy, so the varying needs and capacities of individual kids can be taken into account."

- **Hugh Mackay**

CONTENTS

PROLOGUE

"Mother, will the little prince be there?"

"Yes, my son. He never leaves his mother's side. You will see them all today, if fortune favours us—the good King Henry, his noble queen, to whom he owes so much, and the little prince likewise. We will to horse anon, that we may gain a good view of the procession as it passes. The royal party lodges this night at our good bishop's palace. Perchance they will linger over the Sunday, and hear mass in our fair cathedral, Our loyal folks of Lichfield are burning to show their love by a goodly show of welcome; and it is said that his majesty takes pleasure in silvan sports and such-like simple pleasures, many preparations for the which have been prepared for him to witness."

"O mother, I know. Ralph and Godfrey have been practising themselves this many a day in tilting and wrestling, and in the use of the longbow and quarterstaff, that they may hold their own in the sports on the green before the palace, which they say the king will deign to watch.

"O mother; why am I not as old and as strong as they? I asked Ralph to let me shoot with his bow; but he only laughed at me, and bade me wait till I was as tall and as strong as he. It is very hard to be the youngest—and so much the youngest, too."

The mother smiled as she passed her hand over the floating curls of the gallant boy beside her; He was indeed a child of whom any mother might be proud: beautiful, straight-limbed, active, and fearless, his blue eyes glowing and shining, his cheek flushed with excitement, every look and gesture seeming to speak of the bold soldier spirit that burned within.

And these were times when it appeared indeed as if England's sons had need of all the warlike instincts of their race. Party faction had well-nigh overthrown ere this the throne—and the authority of the meek King Henry, albeit the haughty Duke of York had set forth no claim for the crown, which his son but two short years later both claimed and won. But strife and jealousy and evil purposes were at work in men's minds. The lust of power and of supremacy had begun to pave the way for the civil war which was soon to devastate the land. The sword had already been drawn at St. Albans, and the hearts of many men were full of foreboding as they thought upon the perilous times in which they lived; though others were ready to welcome the strife which promised plunder and glory and fame to those who should distinguish themselves by prowess in field or counsel in the closet.

The gentle Lady Stukely, however, was not one of these. Her heart sank sometimes when she heard the talk of her bold husband and warlike sons. They had all three of them fought for the king at the first battle, or rather skirmish, at St. Albans four years before, and were ardent followers and adherents of the Red Rose of Lancaster. Her husband had received knighthood at the monarch's hands on the eve of the battle, and was prepared to lay down his life in the cause if it should become necessary to do so.

Evelyn Everett-Green

But if rumours of strife to come, and terrible pictures of bloodshed, sometimes made her gentle spirit quail, she had always one consolation in the thought that her youngest child, her little Paul, would not be torn from her side to follow the bloody trail of war. Her two first-born sons, the younger of whom was twenty-two, had long been very finished young gallants, trained to every military enterprise, and eager to unsheathe their swords whenever rumour told of slight to King Henry or his haughty queen from the proud Protector, who for a time had held the reins of government, though exercising his powers in the name of the afflicted king.

But Paul was still a child, not yet quite eight years old; and of the five fair children born to her between him and his brothers, not one had lived to complete his or her third year, so that the mother's heart twined itself the more firmly about this last brave boy, and in the frequent absences of husband and sons upon matters of business or pleasure, the companionship between the pair was almost unbroken, and they loved each other with a devotion that may easily be understood. Paul felt no awe of his gentle mother, but rather looked upon himself as her champion and defender in his father's absence. It was no new thing for him to long for manhood and its privileges; for would not these make him all the stouter protector to his mother?

But she was wont when he spoke such words to check him by gentle counsel and motherly sympathy, and now she took his hand in hers and patted it smilingly as she replied:

"Ah, my little Paul, time flies fast, and you will be a man before very long now; but be content for these next days to be yet a child. Perchance the little prince will pay more heed to such as are of his age.

"You may chance to win a smile from him, even if the nobles

and gentlemen regard not children."

Paul's face brightened instantly.

"O mother, yes; I had not thought of that. But I do so long to see the little prince. Oh, if he were to notice me—to speak to me—how happy I should be! We were born on the same day, were we not, dear mother—on the thirteenth of October? But I am older, am I not?"

"Yes, my child; by two years. You will be eight upon your next birthday, and he six. But I hear he is such a forward, kingly, noble child, that both in appearance and discretion he is far in advance of his actual age. Those who are brought up with royalty early learn the lessons which to others come but with advancing years."

"I love the little prince, our good king's son," cried Paul with kindling eyes; "I would that I had been called Edward, too. Mother, why was I not given his name, as I was born on his day, and that of the good St. Edward too?"

The mother fondly caressed the golden curls of the beautiful child as she answered:

"Ah, my son, we knew not till long afterward that our gracious queen had borne a little son on thy natal day. Paul is a name which many of our race have borne before, and so we called our child by it. It is the man that makes the name, not the name the man."

"I know that, mother; yet I would fain have borne the name of the little prince. But hark! I hear the sounds of the horses' feet. They are bringing them round to the door. Sweet mother, lose no time. Let us mount and depart. I would fain have been in the gallant band of gentlemen who rode out this morning at dawn to welcome and escort the king and queen; as my father and brothers were. But let us not delay. I should be sorely grieved were we to miss seeing the entry into the city."

Lady Stukely smiled at the impatience of the child, knowing well that many hours must elapse before the royal party would reach the city walls; but she was willing to gratify the ardent desires of her little son, and as she was already dressed for the saddle, she rose and took him by the hand and led him out to the courtyard, where some half dozen of the good knight's retainers were awaiting their lady and her son.

Stukely Hall was no very large or pretentious place, but it was built in that quadrangular form so common to that age, and accommodated within its walls the dependents and retainers that every man of rank had about him under the old feudal system, which obliged him to bring to his lord's service on demand a certain following of armed and trained soldiers.

In those days, when every article of common consumption was made at home, the household of even a knight or gentleman of no great wealth or note was no inconsiderable matter, and even the field labourers almost always dwelt within the walls of their lord's house, eating his bread, and growing old in his service as a matter of course, without thinking of such a thing as change.

So that although the greater part of the retainers had ridden off at dawn with the knight and his sons, there were still a good half-dozen stout fellows ready to escort their lady to the town; and besides these were many menials of lower grade standing about to see the start. Little Paul, who had grown up amongst them, ran from one to the other, telling them excitedly how he was going to see the prince that day, and eagerly accepting from the hands of his old nurse a beautiful bunch of red roses which she had gathered that morning, in the hope that her darling might have the chance to offer them to queen or prince.

Mother and son each wore the red rose broidered upon their state robes, and the boy had stuck the crimson blossom in his velvet cap. He was a perfect little picture in his white velvet tunic sloshed with rose colour, his white cloth hosen laced with gold from ankle to thigh, a short cloak flowing jauntily from his shoulders, and his bright golden curls flowing from beneath the crimson and white cap.

No wonder that his stately mother regarded him with looks of fond pride, or that his old nurse breathed a benediction on his pretty head, and invoked the saints and the blessed Virgin on his behalf. They little knew that the gallant child was riding forth to an encounter which would be fraught for him with strange results; and that the long-hoped-for meeting with the little prince would be the first step in one of those passionate attachments which almost always cost the owner of them dear.

The sun shone hot and bright as the little cavalcade set forth from the courtyard. The month was that of July, and merry England was looking its best. The fair landscape lying before the eyes of the riders seemed to breathe nothing but peace and plenty; and it was hard to think that the desolating hand of war might, before many years had passed, be working havoc and ruin over a land so smiling and happy now.

The rich valley in which the ancient city of Lichfield stands looked peculiarly beautiful and fertile that day. Lady Stukely, whilst replying to the eager talk of her excited little boy, could not but gaze around her with admiration, familiar as the scene was to her; and even the boy seemed struck, for

Evelyn Everett-Green

he looked up and said:

"I hope the little prince will be pleased with our town. He will have seen many fine places on this progress, but I do think we shall give him the best welcome of all. We all love him so."

It seemed indeed as if the whole country had turned out to welcome the royal guests; for as the riders drew near to the city walls, they found themselves in the midst of a crowd of holiday folks, all bent upon the same object—namely, to take up a good position for witnessing the royal procession as it passed; and every few minutes some joyous roisterer would raise a shout, "Long live the king!" "Health to the queen!" "Down with the false friends—the House of York!" which cries would be taken up by the multitude, and echoed lustily along the road.

And as the party from Stukely Hall rode up, way being made by the crowd for persons of quality well known and beloved in those parts, little Paul vented his excitement in a new cry of his own; for, standing up in his stirrups and waving his cap in his hand, he cried in his clear boyish tones:

"Three cheers, good people, for the little prince! Three cheers for Edward, Prince of Wales, our future king!"

And this cheer was taken up with hearty goodwill by all the crowd; partly for the sake of the cause ear to the hearts of these loyal people, partly from admiration for the gallant child who had started it; and Paul rode on with a flushed and happy face, looking up to his mother and saying:

"They all love the little prince. Oh how I wish he would come!"

The captain of the little band of soldiers who guarded the gate by which the royal procession was to enter, came forward doffing his mailed head piece to greet the wife of the gallant Sir James, who was a notable gentleman in those parts. By his courtesy the lady and her child were allowed to take up a position so close to the gate as would insure for them a most excellent view of the royal party; whilst the humbler crowd was kept at a more discreet distance by the good-humoured soldiers, who exercised their office amid plenty of jesting and laughing, which showed that an excellent understanding existed between them and their brethren of the soil. The captain, as the hour for the entrance drew near, took up his position beside the lady, and conversed with her in low tones. Paul listened with all his ears the moment he discovered that the soldier was talking about his beloved little prince.

"I do not credit every idle tale I hear, or certes life would be but a sorry thing for a soldier. But there is a queer rumour flying about that some of the bold marauding fellows who follow the banner of York, Salisbury, and Warwick have been following and hanging on the trail of the royal party with a view to the capture—so it is said—of the Prince of Wales, who, once in the hands of the rival faction, would prove a hostage of no mean value. I can scarce credit such a tale myself. Sure am I that it cannot have originated in the mind of any of those noble earls, but must be the device of some meaner churl, who hopes to gain a reward for his treachery. Belike there is no truth whatever in it. Rumour is never idle, and must have some food to satisfy its cravings. I credit not so wild a tale, albeit I must be on the watch against all chances.

"But hark! hear you not that sound in the distance? and methinks I see on yonder height the glitter of the spearmen and the sheen of an armed multitude. Ay, it is truly so. They

14   Evelyn Everett-Green

come, they come! Why, it is a goodly following our gallant knights and gentlemen have furnished. Their gracious majesties will have no cause to grumble at the loyalty of their trusty county of Lichfield {1}."

Paul's breath went and came. The words of the captain had stirred his heart, and now the actual approach of the royal family set every pulse throbbing. Eagerly his eyes were fixed upon the advancing column of gallant riders, the self-appointed bodyguard of the king and queen—a bodyguard which, changing and shifting as the royal party progressed through the kingdom, yet never deserted them throughout the triumphal march, and did not a little to raise within the breast of the queen that martial ardour which was to be so severely tested in days to come.

Nearer and yet more near came the gay procession; banners flying, trumpets sounding, the joy bells from the town giving back gay response. And now the mounted gentlemen—amongst whom Paul's quick eyes have already discovered his father and brothers—wheel rapidly aside to right and left, forming a sort of avenue to the gateway through which the royal riders are to pass, to receive the loyal welcome of the venerable prelate and the city dignitaries.

Paul's breath comes and goes as the cheering in the crowd grows vociferous. He grasps his bunch of roses firmly in his hands, his cheeks glowing till they almost rival the damask bloom of the flowers, his eyes fixed in all their eager brightness upon the advancing band, which consists of the king and queen and prince and their own immediate attendants. It is a moment never forgotten by the boy in after life—the moment when first his glance fell upon the royal child around whose history romance has woven so many a tale; and it was with a start of peculiar surprises and a thrill of emotion he could not have analyzed, that the boy beheld the little prince of his dreams. For in those beautiful princely features, in the alert graceful figure and the floating curls of gold, Paul seemed to see his own lineaments reproduced, and gave one bewildered glance toward his mother to see if perchance the same thought struck her.

And indeed it did; for the chance resemblance between the young heir of the House of Lancaster and the son of an obscure Staffordshire knight was so remarkable that none who saw the two children could fail to be struck by it. Paul for a moment was almost awed, feeling as if he had no right thus to have aped the outward aspect of the little prince; but the next moment all else was forgotten in the excitement of the moment and in the vigorous cheering which greeted the close approach of royalty.

The party moved slowly forward, returning the loyal salutations of the crowd right graciously. The little prince was charming in his friendly gestures, and Paul observed that to one and another of the knights and gentlemen drawn up to do them honour he held out some little token, which was received with every demonstration of respect and gratification.

His intense excitement caused the little Paul to push out somewhat further than the line observed by the soldiers, and no one recalled him to his place; and thus it was that when, as the cortege moved forward, the Prince of Wales dropped the plumed hat with the white ostrich feather, which he was raising in response to the salutations showered upon him, it was Paul who had leaped to the ground and caught up the costly headgear from beneath the very feet of the king's horse, and, with glowing face and ardent gaze of admiration and homage, had bent the knee to the princely child, and restored the cap, whilst his bunch of roses was offered at the same moment with an air of modest eagerness that touched

Evelyn Everett-Green

all hearts.

The little prince took both the cap and the flowers, thanking the lad with friendly smiles; but when he saw how closely that bright face resembled his own, and how those floating curls of shining gold uncovered to the hot sunshine were but as the counterpart of his, he too glanced at his mother, whose smiling face was bent with a proud pleasure upon the pretty picture formed by the two children, and he said in his clear, joyous tones:

"Why, verily, this must be a brother or a cousin of mine own. Tell me your name, good lad. Surely we must be akin."

"Nay, gracious prince," answered Paul in low tones; "I am but the son of a simple knight, who has ever been your royal father's loyal servant. But I was born, like you, upon St. Edward's Day, and perhaps our patron saint smiled kindly on us both."

The boy was so excited he scarce knew what he said; but his words seemed to please the little prince, who replied:

"Nay, now, if you share the good offices of my patron saint, you must wear my badge too, for love of me. See here, this little silver swan, the device of my noble ancestor King Edward the Third, it is now my badge, and you must wear it for my sake. Farewell for the nonce; we shall meet again—I am sure of it—ere we say goodbye to this pleasant city. I would I had a brother like you. But we will meet anon. Farewell, and forget me not."

The royal cavalcade was yet moving onward whilst these gracious words of childish greeting were spoken. The next moment the bewildered Paul was standing looking after the pretty child prince, the silver swan he grasped tightly between his hands alone convincing him that the whole encounter had not been a fair fleeting dream.

The great green meadow just without the walls of the city presented an animated spectacle even to eyes accustomed to the gay and party-coloured dresses of the Middle Ages, and to the hardy sports of her bold sons. The whole town and countryside had assembled to witness or bear a share in the merry silvan sports, instituted with a view of amusing the royal guests, who had halted at Lichfield for three nights in order that the pious monarch might hear mass on Sunday at the cathedral; and the Saturday was given over to the revels and pastimes at all times dear to the people, but more so than ever when royalty deigned to be the witness of the feats of skill and strength. And King Henry loved to watch the sports of his subjects. His simple mind; that shrank from the intrigues of court life, seemed to gather strength and health when removed from the strife and turmoil of parties. His malady, which at times completely incapacitated him from tasking part in the government, was always liable to recur, and it was with a view of recuperating his health, and calming his anxieties and fears for himself and those he loved best, that the queen had decided upon this progress through the loyal midland counties, and encouraged the people to display their skill in manly sports before their king; for nothing seemed more beneficial to him than the interest evoked by any spectacles of this kind.

And little Paul Stukely was an eager spectator of the encounters and feats that were taking place before royalty that bright summer day. Paul felt as if he were living and moving in a wonderful dream. He kept pulling off his little velvet cap to make sure that the silver swan—the prince's token—was still in its place; and even when most interested in any contest going on upon the green, his eyes would turn instinctively toward the fair child leaning upon his father's

Evelyn Everett-Green

knee, and eagerly watching the rustic revels.

The royal guests were sumptuously lodged beneath a silken awning under a mighty oak tree that gave a refreshing shade. A platform had been erected for them beneath the awning, and chairs of state set thereon. From this vantage ground they could watch everything that went on, and reward the victors with words of praise, small pieces of silver, or some fragment of lace or ribbon from the royal apparel, as best suited the rank of the aspirant for honour; and the kindly smiles and gracious words bestowed upon all who approached increased each hour the popularity of the Lancastrian cause and the devotion of the people to their king.

But Paul had not, so far, ventured to present himself before the platform where the little prince was standing. He had not forgotten a single one of the kind words spoken by the youthful Edward yesterday, but he was fearful of presuming upon the favour thus shown him, and his very admiration for the princely child seemed to hold him back.

He knew that his father and brothers might rebuke him for forwardness if he presumed to thrust himself into notice. Sir James was one of those appointed to keep order upon the ground, and withhold the rustics from incommoding in any way the royal visitors; and the child knew that he would be the first to rebuke his own son for putting himself unduly forward. As the youngest in the house, Paul was accustomed to be held in small repute, and had no desire to provoke a rebuff which might even reach the ears of the little prince himself.

So he contented himself by hanging about on the outskirts of the crowd, casting many longing, lingering glances toward the group beneath the giant oak, and at other times diverting himself by watching the wrestlers, the mummers, or the archers, who in turn came forward to try their skill and strength. The quarterstaff contests were very exciting, and several broken heads were the result of the hearty encounters with that formidable weapon.

But Paul was familiar with most of the sports, and presently grew weary of watching. It was hot, too, and there was not much shade to be had in that big meadow; so he wandered a little apart, toward a copse beside a small stream, on the opposite side of which a thick forest rose stately and grand, and sitting down beside the merry brook, he clasped his hands round his knees and sank into a reverie.

He was so engrossed in his thoughts that he did not notice the light tread of approaching footsteps, and gave a great start when he suddenly felt an arm flung caressingly about his neck. He sprang to his feet with a cry of astonishment, and stood face to face with the little prince.

"You see I have found you," cried the child gleefully. "I saw you several times in the crowd today, but you would not come near me. Never mind; this is much better, for here we can talk, here we can be friends. Are you aweary of their gay shows? So am I, in faith. We have seen the same thing everywhere, and it is so good to be alone sometimes. I love not to be always followed and watched.

"See you that dim, dark wood? Let us e'en hide ourselves therein for a short hour. My mother will miss me from her side anon, and will send to seek me. I would not be found too easily. Come, let us hide ourselves there, and you shall tell me all about yourself, and we will play at being trusty friends and comrades.

"It is dull work being always a prince. I would that we could change parts for once. You shall be the prince and I will be

Evelyn Everett-Green

the bold knight's son, and your very faithful servant."

"O my lord!" faltered Paul, almost overcome with excitement and pleasure at this strange encounter.

But the little prince stamped his foot and spoke with the air of a regular little autocrat.

"Nay, call me not that. Did I not say I would be nobody's lord for the nonce? What is your name? Paul? Then I will be called Paul for this next hour, and you shall be Edward. See, here is my jewelled collar and the cap with the ostrich plume—the badge of the Prince of Wales. Yes, put them on, put them on. Marry, I could think it was my very self, but a short inch the taller.

"Now, see, I take your cap instead; and now I am Paul, and you must bid me follow you and attend you in your journey through the forest. See, we will be fugitives, flying from the wicked Duke of York, who would fain grasp at the king's power, but my mother will not let him."

For a moment the child's eyes flashed, and his clenched hands and heaving breast showed that the spirit of Margaret of Anjou lived again in her child; but pulling himself up short with a laugh, the little prince added with a deferential bow, resuming his character of subject, "But I crave your pardon, sweet prince, if I lose control of myself in the thought of your wrongs. Lead on, noble lord, and I follow. Let us seek safety in the dim aisles of yon giant wood. Surely there is some ford or bridge nigh at hand which will give us safe crossing without wetting ourselves."

Children are children all the world over, and at any period of its history. Childhood ever delights in romance and imaginative situations and adventures; and before ten minutes had passed the boys had completely entered into the spirit of their play. Paul, shaking off the awe which had at first held him silent and abashed, played the part of prince with an energy and zeal which evoked the delight and admiration of his companion; whilst the younger boy was amused to lay aside for the moment any pretence at royalty, and pay his humble devoirs to his liege lord.

Paul knew of some stepping stones which led across the stream into the dark wood, and soon the boys were in what seemed to them the heart of the great forest. The prince was delighted by all he saw. The sense of freedom was enchanting, and his curiosity unbounded. He had never in his life before enjoyed a game of play in so unfettered a fashion with a comrade of nearly his own age; and soon forgetting even their own game, the boys were walking with arms twined round each other's neck, telling each other all that was in their hearts, and exchanging vows of unalterable affection.

"When I am grown to manhood, and am a belted knight with noble gentlemen of mine own to attend me, you shall be my very first esquire, Paul," said the prince emphatically; "and we will ride through the world together, seeking adventures which shall make all men wonder when they hear of them. And when I am king you shall be my first counsellor and greatest lord. I will degrade from office and dignity those proud nobles who have been traitors at heart to my kingly father, and to you I will give their broad lands and high titles. We will thus be comrades and friends through life. You would never desert me, would you, Paul?"

"I would lay down my life for your highness," cried Paul with enthusiasm. "I will live and die true to the Red Rose— to the sign of the silver swan."

The little prince's eyes kindled.

"I believe you would. I love you, Paul, and methinks that you would love me too. I would that I could take you with me now to be my friend and comrade through life; but perchance your lady mother could ill spare you, by what you say. I know what a mother's love is like."

Paul's face was grave. For the first time in his life he was confronted by the problem of a divided duty—that problem which troubles us all more or less at some time in our history.

"I would gladly go with your highness to the world's end," he said. "I should love to live and die at your side; but I doubt me if it would not be cruel to my mother. She sometimes tells me that her life would be a lone one without me."

"And you must stay with her," said the prince with decision; "at least so long as you are a child. When you are a grown man it will be different. Some day I will send for you, and you shall be my first and best friend; but it cannot be now. My mother might not approve my choice, and yours might not let you go. Princes as well as other men have to wait for what they want"—and the child sighed—"but some day our turn will come."

Then they resumed their play, and the hoary wood resounded to the merry shouts of the boys as they ran hither and thither in active sport, till the little prince was fairly tired out, though, still exulting in his escape from maternal vigilance, he stoutly protested against going back.

"See, good Paul," he said, "here is a right commodious hollow tree, heaped with last year's dead leaves. I will rest awhile hidden away here, where none will find me were they to look for me ever so. And if you could find and bring me here a draught of water from the brook or from some spring, I should be ever grateful. I am sore athirst and weary, too."

The child was nevertheless much pleased with his nest, and forthwith curled himself up in it like a young dormouse, delighting in the conviction that no attendants despatched by his mother to capture him would ever find him here. Boys have been young pickles ever since the world began, and were just as full of pranks in the fifteenth century as they are now. Edward had: a full share of boyhood's mischievous delight in his own way, and owing to the strong will and the ever-present vigilance of his mother, he had not had many chances of indulging his natural craving for independence. Therefore he rejoiced the more in it now, and was quite determined to return to his royal parents at such time only as it suited his own whim.

Paul was willing enough to do the behest of the prince, and stayed only to make him comfortable before starting off on the quest for water. He thought young Edward would soon be asleep, as indeed he was, so luxurious was his leafy couch within the giant oak; and resolved to run as far as a certain well he knew of in the wood, the water of which was peculiarly fresh and cold and clear, and where a cup was always kept by the brothers of a neighbouring monastery for the benefit of weary travellers.

Paul sped away on his mission with a light heart He was elated above measure by his day's adventure, and his head was brimming over with plans and dreams of the future, which was to be so glorious and so distinguished.

He the chosen comrade of their future king! he the loyal upholder of that king's rights, the bulwark of the throne, the trusted noble, the shrewd counsellor, the valiant warrior! A

Evelyn Everett-Green

boy's ambition is boundless—innocent of envy or evil, but wild in its flights.

Paul went on his way with glowing cheeks and sparkling eyes, till a stealthy sound in the bushes beside him made him stop short, listening intently. He heard voices in cautious whisper.

"He cannot be far away. He certainly came to the wood. Long Peter says he had another boy with him; but be that as it may, he is here, and close at hand. We must lose no time. The alarm will be given if he is missed. Take one, or take both, it matters not if we but get the prince into our hands. He may be known by his ostrich plume and his golden curls, and the jewelled collar he wears about his neck."

Paul heard these words plainly, and it seemed as if his heart were in his mouth. It beat so violently that he fancied the conspirators must surely hear. The words he had heard but yesterday flashed back into his mind.

It was true then. There was a conspiracy to carry off the young prince, and the band of men pledged to the deed were actually on their track and close at hand. How could he warn the prince in time? How could he save him from their hands?

For a moment the boy's courage seemed to desert him. A cold sweat broke out on his face, his knees trembled beneath him. But his fear was not a selfish or unworthy one; it was all for the royal child, whose peril was so imminent.

And then, with a sudden revulsion of feeling, he recollected that he himself wore the cap with the white plume, the jewelled collar of royalty, and the dagger the little prince habitually carried in his girdle. And had he not the same floating golden curls, the same cast of features, the same active figure, and almost the same stature? Might he not save the real prince by playing his part to some purpose for the time being? The men would not distinguish between the pair—he felt certain of that; they would at once make off with their prize. Later on, of course, they would discover the trick, but then the prince would be safe. His own followers would have long since discovered him. Yes, he would do it—he would save the prince at all cost. What did it matter if his own life were the forfeit? The heir of England would be saved.

It was no small act of heroism to which the boy made up his mind in those few moments. Those were lawless days, and human life was held very cheap. The band of fierce men who had believed they were carrying off a prince, would think nothing of running him through with their swords when they discovered how they had been tricked, and that by a mere child. Paul set his teeth hard and braced himself up for the task he had set himself. He knew his peril-he realized it too; but he was a soldier's son, and had he not said he would live and die for the prince? Would he ever be worthy of the knighthood every lad looked forward to as the goal of his ambition, if he shrank now from the task he had set himself?

Hardly had that resolution been taken before there sprang out from the thick underwood two or three fierce-looking men, armed to the teeth.

"Ha, my young springal! well met, in sooth," cried the foremost of the band, laying a firm hand upon the boy's shoulder. "We have been looking long for you.

"To horse, brave fellows! we have our prize. We may not linger here."

"Hands off, varlet!" cried Paul, throwing himself into the character of prince with great energy and goodwill. "Know

Evelyn Everett-Green

you to whom you speak—whom ye thus rough handle? Have a care; the Prince of Wales is not thus to be treated."

"Pardon, sweet prince," cried the leader, with ironical courtesy, his grasp not relaxing one whit from the boy's arm. "Time leaves us scant opportunity for the smooth speech of the court. We must use all despatch in conveying your worshipful presence hence, to the safe custody of England's friends.

"Nay, struggle not, boy. We would not harm you. You are safe with us—"

"I know you not. I will not be thus insulted. I will to my royal parents," cried Paul in well-feigned indignation.

But remonstrance and resistance were alike useless. At the sound of a peculiar whistle from one of the party, there immediately appeared some half score of mounted troopers, leading other horses with them. The boy was swung upon the saddle of one of the horses and fastened there by means of thongs, which, although not incommoding him whilst riding, utterly precluded all idea of escape. Moreover the steed was placed between those of two of the stalwart troopers, each of whom kept a hand upon the reins of the supposed prince; and thus, silently but rapidly, the little band threaded the intricacies of the wood, by paths evidently known to them, and ere the dusk had fully come, had cleared the forest altogether, and were galloping steadily and fast across the open country toward the north.

Paul had not spoken another word. He had been in terror lest by some inadvertent phrase he might betray himself, and let those fierce men know that he was not the prince; in which case not only might his own life be forfeit, but the real prince might fall into their hands. But now as the dusk overtook them, and still they were flying farther and farther away from the city where the prince lay, his heart rose, and beat with a generous triumph; for though his own fate might be a speedy death, the heir of England was safe.

It was dark before the lights of a wayside hostelry became visible across the dreary waste they were traversing. The leader of the band turned and addressed a few words to the troopers who had the care of the captive; and at once he felt himself deprived of the tell-tale cap and collar, the former of which was replaced by a cloth cap belonging to one of the men, which almost concealed the boy's features. He was also wrapped in a mantle that further disguised him; and thus they rode up to the inn.

A ruddy stream of light poured out from that comfortable hostelry, and Paul saw, seated on his stout nag, with three of his servants behind him, the well-known figure of a neighbouring farmer, whom business often took to a town many miles from his native place.

The troopers were dismounting and hurrying into the inn. Two only remained with their prize. Paul's resolution was quickly taken. He threw off the encumbering mantle and cap, and cried aloud:

"Gaffer Hood, Gaffer Hood, come and help me! These men have carried me off, and are taking me I know not whither. Come and help me to get free, and my father will richly reward you. They think I am the Prince of Wales, who was playing with me but this afternoon. Tell them who I really am, and they will let me go."

"By the mass, if that be not the voice of little Paul Stukely!" exclaimed the honest farmer in great amazement, as he brought his stout nag alongside the animal that carried the

Evelyn Everett-Green

child. The troopers drew their swords as if to interpose (and in those days it was considered better to leave these reckless gentlemen alone when they had booty in their hands, however come by, and no doubt they were in league with the host of the inn); but the character of the dialogue between the farmer and the child was so astounding that the men remained mute and motionless, whilst the leader of the gang, who had heard something of the words, came hurrying to the spot, to see that his prize was safe.

He was quite prepared to make short work of farmer and men alike if there should be any futile attempt at rescue. The man knew his trade, and long habit had made him utterly reckless of human life. But the words he heard exchanged between the child and the farmer held him spellbound, too.

"I was playing with the prince," cried Paul, loud enough for all to hear. "He bid me take his collar and cap and be prince in fantasy, whilst he was my esquire. Afterwards, when he was weary, he lay down to rest, and these fellows caught me and carried me off, thinking I was prince indeed. I would not tell them what they had done, lest they should return and capture him. But bid them loose me now, good Gaffer, and give them all the money in your pouch as my ransom, and I warrant my father will repay you double.

"It is the heir of the House of Lancaster you want, gentlemen, not a poor knight's youngest son, a lad of no account. This good man will pay you some broad gold pieces if you will let me go; but if you are resolved to take my life as the price of my deceit, why, take it now. I am not afraid to die in a good cause, and this worthy man will perchance take home my body to my mother, that it may lie in time beside hers."

"Nay, lad, we will all die ere they shall touch a hair of thy bonny head," cried the honest farmer, signing to his men to come and be ready. "If there's a man in this troop dastard enough to lay a hand upon thee, he shall settle accounts with Gaffer Hood ere he leaves the place. A farmer can fight, ay, and give good strong blows, too.

"Now, gentlemen, which of you will lay hands on that gallant child? for he will have to do it across my dead body first."

"Tush, man, put up thy sword," cried the leader of the band, who, being a man prompt both in action and thought, had taken in the bearings of the situation with great rapidity, and upon whom the simple heroism of the child had not been thrown away.

Rough and self-seeking and cruel as lawless times had made such men, they were not devoid of all better feelings; and although, had there been no interposition on his behalf, Paul might have been a victim to their irritation at being thus duped, as it was his life was now safe enough.

"We war not with babes and children. The boy has borne himself gallantly, and we will take the gold pieces and let him go free. Our chance may come another time, and we want not the cumbrance of children on our march. He would not be hostage worth having, so ransom him and begone. We have the prince's jewels if we have not the lad himself.

"Go your way, boy; you will make a soldier in time. You have the right grit in you. Farewell! one day we may meet again."

And thinking, perhaps, that he and his band had better not linger longer, the captain gave the word to mount; and as soon as Paul's thongs were cut and the ransom paid over, the troopers set spurs to their horses' sides and vanished away in the darkness.

Once again little Paul Stukely stood in the presence of royalty. The prince's arm was about his neck, the proud queen's eyes—moist now with tears—were bent upon him in loving gratitude, whilst from the king's lips he was receiving words of praise that set the hot blood mounting to his brow. Behind him stood his father, all around were the attendants of the royal family; and Paul, unaccustomed to be thus the centre of attention, almost wished the ground would open to hide him, although his heart could not but beat high in gratification and loving loyalty.

All the city was ringing with the daring attempt that had been made to carry off the young Prince of Wales, and the gallantry of the boy who had dared to brave the consequences, and take upon himself the personality of the youthful Edward. The child himself, the farmer who had been the means of his restoration, and the knight who owned so brave a son, all had been heroes of the past six-and-thirty hours.

A special mass of thanksgiving had been sung in the cathedral on the Sunday. The captain of the town, who had heard a rumour which had sent him flying into the forest the previous afternoon, to find the true prince vainly seeking his missing comrade, could not make enough of the boy whose simple-hearted gallantry had saved him from a lasting remorse, and perhaps a lasting disgrace. Indeed, Sir James Stukely had had to hurry his child home in haste to his mother's care, lest he should hear too much of his own prowess; and, thrusting him into her loving arms, had said, in a voice which quivered in spite of himself:

"Here, dame, take the boy and give him a kiss to show that he has been a good lad. He has done his duty, as a Stukely ought to do, and that should be enough for all of us. But let us have no nonsense talked. What will the country come to if everyone who does his duty as it should be done expects to be called a hero, and I know not what besides? The prince is safe, and the boy likewise. Now off to bed with him, and no more nonsense to be talked in my hearing.

"God bless you, child! You'll live yet to be a credit to the name you bear."

And Paul was made happier by that one word from his stern though loving sire than by all the praises he had heard lavished upon himself during the past hours. For there was no one in the wide world that the child so reverenced as his dark-browed father, who seldom praised his children, and was inflexible in his punishments whenever they were deserved. To be told by him that he had done his duty, and would be a credit to his house, was happiness far beyond his deserts, he thought; and he registered a mental vow, deep down in his brave little heart, that he would never in time to come give the world cause to say he had not lived up to the promise of his boyhood.

The loving sympathy with which his mother listened to his story, the caresses she showered upon him in thought of the deadly peril in which he had stood, and the hearty approbation of his brothers and the retainers and servants in his father's halls, were a small pleasure as compared with those few brief, almost stern, words from that father himself. Even the notification that he was to present himself on the Monday before the king and queen added little to his happiness, although the idea of seeing once again his admired little prince could not but fill him with gratification.

His father led him to the royal presence, and bowed low on hearing himself thanked for having brought up sons who so well demonstrated the loyalty and devotion which had been

Evelyn Everett-Green

born and bred in them. But Paul scarce heard what passed, for the little prince dashed forward to take him round the neck, kissing him with all the natural grace of childhood, whilst half rebuking him for having denied him his own legitimate share in the adventure.

"If we had but been together we would have achieved our own liberty," he said, his bright eyes flashing with the spirit of his ancestors. "We would have shown them what Plantagenet blood could do. I would I had been there. I would I had shared the adventure with you. It would have been a thing for our bards to write of, for our soldiers to sing over their campfires. But now I shall have none of the glory. I was sleeping in a tree. It was you who were the hero, the prince."

"Ah, sweet prince, had they once laid hold on the true prize, methinks neither you nor I would so easily have escaped," said Paul, who had vivid recollections of the iron hands that had been laid upon him by the stern men who had carried him off. "I know not how I could have escaped, had it not been that they were willing to be quit of me when they found out I was not him whom they sought."

But the prince was hardly satisfied with the rather tame ending to the adventure.

"To be rescued by a farmer, and carried home on his nag!" he said, tossing back his curls with a gesture of hauteur. "Paul, I would that you had cut your way through the very heart of them. I would you had left at least one or two dead upon the spot. Had we been together—" He clenched his hands for a moment, but then laughed a little, and said in a whisper—"But no matter, Paul; they all say that you played the hero, and I will not envy you for it. We shall be men one day, and then I shall come and claim your promise. You will be my faithful esquire, and I will be your liege lord. Together we will roam the world in search of adventure, and well I know that we shall meet with such as will not disgrace the royal house of the Plantagenet."

The child's eyes flashed, and an answering spark was kindled in the breast of the hardy little Paul. He put his hand within that of the prince, and cried loud enough to be heard by those who stood by:

"Dear my lord, I will serve you to the death. I will go with you to the world's end."

Sir James laid a warning hand upon his son's shoulder.

"Boy," he said in a low voice, "it becomes thee not thus to put thyself forward in the presence of royalty. Be silent before thy betters, and show thy loyalty by thy deeds, not by high-sounding words of which thou canst have but little understanding."

Paul was instantly abashed. Indeed, in those days it was not usual for children to make their voices heard in the presence of their elders; but the prince was privileged, and it was his words that had drawn forth this exclamation from Paul.

The king and the queen, however, smiled upon the boy; and the latter said in tender tones, that would have amazed some amongst her enemies:

"Nay, chide not the boy, good Sir James; he does but speak as his heart dictates, and I would indeed that my son might look forward to the day when he and your gallant son might be companions in arms. But I ask no pledge in these troublous, stormy days. Only I will cherish the hope that when brighter days dawn for the House of Lancaster, and her

Evelyn Everett-Green

proud foes are forever subjugated to their right position, this bold boy may appear again before us to receive at our hands the guerdon he is too young for yet. And be sure that never will knighthood be more gladly accorded to any than to him, for the deed which saved England's heir and hope from the deadly peril which menaced him but a few short hours ago."

Sir James and his son both bowed low, and the father prepared to lead away the boy. But the prince had once more thrown his arms round Paul's neck, and was speaking in his eager way:

"You and I will be knighted together when we are grown. I shall think of you, and you will not forget me—promise that you will not. And when we meet next, wherever it may be, we shall know each other for the likeness we bear the one to the other. Kiss me, Paul, and promise never to forget. Farewell now, but my heart tells me we shall meet again."

The king's son and the knight's embraced with all the warmth of a real and deep affection, albeit of only a few hours' growth, and gazing at each other to the last they parted.

"I shall always wear the silver swan," Paul had said as their lips met. "You will know me by that. And I—oh, I never could forget you! Your face will live always in my heart."

The doors closed behind the retiring knight and his son. The vision alone conjured up by the words of the prince lived in the heart of Paul Stukely. His face was very brightly grave as he rode home beside his father. How little he or any in that noble company guessed where and under what circumstances the prince and Paul would meet next!

CHAPTER 1

A BRUSH WITH THE ROBBERS

"Help—help—help!"

This cry, growing feebler at each repetition, was borne by the evening breeze to the ears of a traveller who was picking his way along the dark mazes of Epping Forest one cool, fresh October day. Instinctively he drew rein and listened, laying his band unconsciously upon the hilt of his poniard.

"A woman's voice," he said half aloud, as he spurred more rapidly onward in the direction whence the cry proceeded. "A woman set upon, no doubt, by some band of these marauders who are desolating the country and disgracing humanity. Cowards! I wonder how many of them there are? A solitary traveller has not much chance against a gang of them; but at least I can sell my life dear. I have little enough to live for now; and it would be a stain for ever upon my father's fame were I to pass by unheeding the cry of a damsel in distress.

"Forward, then, good Sultan; there is work for both of us before we can think of food or lodging after our weary day of travel. Forward, good horse."

Evelyn Everett-Green

The coal-black charger, who, despite his jaded air and look of neglect, had evidently come of a good stock, and had both blood and mettle of the true soldier sort in him, pricked his ears, arched his neck, and appeared to be fully aware of what was required of him by his loved master. He broke into a gentle canter, and despite the roughness of the ground, maintained that pace for several hundred yards, until the hand of the traveller upon his rein warned him to moderate his pace.

The shades of evening were falling fast, but a young moon rode high in the sky, and helped to light up the expanse of broken ground and piled-up tree trunks which suddenly became visible to the traveller as he reached a clearing in the forest, through which the rough trail or path he was pursuing led. And here in this clearing he came upon the object of his search, and saw that his surmise as to the cause of the cries he had heard was only too correct. Four big burly men, all armed with the weapons of the day—bills, maces, and even the handgun, which was beginning to find a place amongst the more time-honoured arms of offence and defence—were surrounding the struggling figure of a woman, a young woman the traveller fancied, from her slimness and the cat-like agility which she displayed in struggling with her captors.

It appeared as if the men did not desire to hurt her if they could avoid doing so, but rather wished to make of her a prisoner; whilst she was making the most frantic efforts to escape from their restraining hands, and was uttering strangled cries for help, which were so deadened by the thick folds of the heavy driving cloak, which had been wrapped about her head, as to be barely audible even at a short distance.

"Let her fight and struggle," said a tall, broad-shouldered man with a darkly sinister face, who stood a little apart all this while, keeping, however, a very close watch upon the group. "She will soon tire herself out, and then we can carry her away peacefully. Don't hurt her. Let her have her fling— it won't last long—and she will be all the tamer afterward."

The traveller, who was but a stripling himself, set his teeth hard as he heard these words spoken. Something in the cool arrogance of the man, who appeared to be a leader of the rest, stirred his blood and made his hands tingle to be at his throat.

But it would not do to act rashly in an encounter with four stalwart men, all armed to the teeth, and plainly well used to the practice of arms. The youth saw that he must husband his strength and use his opportunity with every care. His best chance lay in taking the party by surprise.

He examined his weapons with a keen eye. He too possessed one of the handguns of the period, and was a good marksman to boot. He had, too—and glad enough was he of it at that moment—the deadly guisarme, that old-fashioned weapon that combined a spear and scythe, and was used with horrible effect in the charges of the day. Then there was the short battle-axe, slung across his saddlebow, which at close quarters would be a formidable weapon, and the poniard in his belt had in its time done deadly work before this.

But although he had plenty of weapons for offence, he had not much defensive armour upon him. Only a cloth cap protected his head, and although his jerkin was of the tough leather which often defied the thrust of a dagger almost as successfully as mail, it might not prove a defence against the combined attack of a number of enemies; and his legs were unprotected save by the long leather riding boots laced up the front, and ornamented with silken tassels, now much faded and stained.

Evelyn Everett-Green

Altogether, he appeared hardly equipped for so desperate an encounter as the one that lay before him; but it was plain that he did not on that account shrink from it. His appearance upon the scene had not been observed by any of the robbers—for such they plainly were—and he was thus able to take his time and weigh his chances carefully.

The girl was suffering no injury from her captors; but what her fate might be if rescue did not come was what no one could say. It was plain that it was the desire of the leader of the band to possess her as a captive. It was he who was the leading spirit in the attack. He was just as determined to carry her off as he was wishful to accomplish the capture without inflicting injury.

The stripling astride the good warhorse—who seemed to scent battle in the air, and stood perfectly still, quivering with excitement—unslung his handgun from his shoulder, and levelled it at the leader of the band. The next instant a sharp report rang through the silent forest. The robber chief flung up his hands with a stifled cry and sank down upon the ground; whilst the other men, astonished beyond measure at this sudden attack from they knew not what quarter, ceased to heed their prisoner, and turned round with loud execrations, laying their hands upon their weapons.

But before they had time to draw these the horseman was upon them. He had his battle-axe in his hand—a light small axe, but one of exquisite temper and workmanship—and dashing through the group, he dealt such a blow with it upon the head of one of the ruffians as cleft his skull in two; and the man dropped with never a groan, a dead corpse upon the ground.

"Two done for," quoth the youth to himself as he wheeled about for a second encounter. "Well, a mounted man should be a match for two on foot.

"Ha! what is that?" for even as he spoke he felt a sharp, stinging pain in one shoulder, and simultaneously the report of firearms rang out once more. His adversaries had not been slow to avenge the death of their comrade, and their aim was as true as his own. The traveller knew that his only chance was now to close with his foes and grapple with them before they could load their piece again.

His right arm was partially disabled, as he felt in a moment. He could no longer swing the trusty little axe which had done good service before; but there was the deadly guisarme at his side. Sultan could be trusted to carry him straight to the foe without any guidance beyond that of the pressure of knee and foot; and grasping the weapon in both hands, he gallantly charged back upon the men, who stood grimly awaiting his next movement with every intention of unhorsing and slaying him.

The odds were heavy against him. The two ruffians who stood to bar his way were stalwart, powerful fellows, well inured to this kind of warfare; and the chief, who though wounded was not killed, had struggled to his feet, and was plainly endeavouring, though with difficulty, to reach the handgun and reload it. The girl was still encumbered by the heavy cloak which had been knotted about her head and hands, and was not at once thrown off. The traveller plainly saw that there was no time to be lost if he was to escape with his own life, or save the damsel from a fate perhaps worse than death.

"Forward, Sultan!" he cried.

And the good horse dashed back upon the enemy; and the youth, holding his weapon in both hands, strove as he passed to deal a deadly blow to one of his assailants. But the man was quick, and his own strength impaired by the injury he had received. The lance-like point of the weapon inflicted a deep gash upon the face of one of his adversaries, causing him to yell with rage and pain, but no vital injury had been inflicted upon either; whilst a savage blow from the other upon the youth's left arm had broken the bone, and he felt as if his last moment had surely come.

But it did not occur to him even then to save himself by flight, as he could well have done, seeing that he was mounted and that the robbers were on foot. Disabled as he was, he wheeled about once more, and half maddened by pain and the desperation of his case, rode furiously upon the only man who had not yet received some injury. The robber awaited his charge with a smile of triumph upon his face; but he triumphed a little too soon.

Sultan was a horse of remarkable intelligence and fidelity. He had known fighting before now—had carried his rider through many a skirmish before this; and his fidelity and affection equalled his intelligence. With the wonderful instinct that seems always to exist between horse and rider who have known each other long, he appeared to divine that his master's case was somewhat desperate, and that he needed an ally in his cause. And thus when the pair bore down upon the robber, who was coolly awaiting the charge, Sultan took law into his own hands, and overthrew the plan both of attack and defence by a quick movement of his own. For he swerved slightly as he approached the man, and rising suddenly upon his hind legs, brought down all the weight of his iron shoe with tremendous force upon the head of the adversary, who fell to the ground with a low groan, and lay as helpless as his former comrade.

But excellent as this manoeuvre was in one aspect, it

disconcerted the rider by its suddenness; and when as the horse reared the second robber sprang upon the rider to try and drag him from his seat, the effort was only too successful. The traveller was easily pulled away from the saddle, and fell heavily to the ground; whilst the foe uttered a savage exclamation of triumph, and knelt with his knee upon the chest of the fallen man, his bloody and distorted visage bent over him in evil triumph. He was feeling in his belt for his dagger; and the young man closed his eyes and tried to mutter a prayer, for he knew that his hour had come at last.

He had sold his life dear, but sold it was, and the next moment he felt certain would be his last; when all in a moment there was another of those loud reports of the gun. The man kneeling upon his chest fell suddenly backwards; and the youth, starting to his feet, was confronted by the spectacle of the maiden he had rescued, white and trembling, and almost overcome by her own deed, holding in her hand the still smoking gun, whilst her eyes, dilated with horror, were fixed upon the helpless creature in the dust.

"Is he dead?" she asked in a hollow voice.

"I cannot tell," answered the youth hastily. "It were better not to linger longer here. Their own band will come and look to them if they return not by sundown. Let us to horse and away before any of the gang come. Sultan will carry the pair of us well, and you will tell us which course to steer; for the night will be upon us ere long, and I am a stranger to these dark forests."

Whilst thus speaking, the traveller was throwing keen glances round him, and saw that the men, though wounded, were not all dead—though one certainly was, and the other, whom Sultan had attacked, was scarce likely to look again upon the light of day. The leader of the band had fallen again to the earth, and was enveloped in the folds of the heavy cloak, from which he appeared to be feebly struggling to disentangle himself. The girl followed the direction of the youth's glance, and explained the matter in a few short words.

"He was loading the gun when I freed myself. I knew that he was going to shoot you. I am very strong, and I saw that he was bleeding and wounded. I sprang upon him and threw him down, and tied the cloak about him, as he had bidden his men bind it about me, By that time you were unhorsed, and I saw that the robber was about to kill you. The gun was loaded, and I took it and shot him. I never killed a man before. I hope it is not wicked; but he would have killed you else. And you had risked your life a dozen times to save me."

"It was well and bravely done for me and for yourself," answered the stranger, as he mounted the docile Sultan and assisted the girl to spring up behind him.

Wounded and spent as he was, the excitement of the encounter had not yet subsided, and he was only vaguely conscious of his hurts, whilst he was very much in earnest in his desire to get away from this ill-omened spot before others of the band should return in search of their missing comrades, and take a terrible vengeance upon those who had slain or wounded them.

His companion was no less anxious than he to be gone; and as the good horse picked his way in the dim light through the intricate forest paths pointed out by the girl, who was plainly a native of the neighbourhood, she told him in whispers of the men from whom she had escaped, and of the fate which had so narrowly overtaken her.

"They are the robbers of Black Notley," she said. "There are two rival bands of robbers here—one at White Notley and one at Black Notley. We call them the Black or the White Robbers, to distinguish between them. The White are not so fierce or so lawless as the Black; but both are a terror to us, for we never know what violence we shall not hear of next."

"And these Black Robbers would have carried you away with them, by what I gathered from their words, at least from the words of him they looked to as their leader?"

The girl shuddered strongly.

"Once he lived in our village—Much Waltham, as it is called. He was no robber then; but a proper youth enough; and although I was but a little maid, not grown to womanhood, he asked my hand of my father in marriage."

"And what said your father to his suit?"

"Why, that I was too young to be betrothed as yet; but that if he were a steady youth, as time went on perchance it might be even as he wished. But instead of growing up to the plough or the anvils as other youths of our village do, he must needs go off to see somewhat of the wars; and when he returned it was as a swashbuckler and roisterer, such as my father and mother cannot abide sight of. When he came to Figeon's to ask me in marriage, he was turned from the door with cold looks and short words; but he would ever be striving to see me alone, and swear that he loved me and would wed me in spite of all. I had liked him when I was but a child, but I grew first to fear and then to hate him; and at last I spoke to Will Ives, the smith's son, of how he troubled me and gave me no peace of my life. And forthwith there was a great stir through the village; and Will Ives set upon him and beat him within an inch of his life, for all he was so proud of his skill and strength. And the good brothers spoke

Evelyn Everett-Green

to him seriously of his evil courses, and I know not what besides. So the end was that he ran away once more and joined himself to the Robbers of Black Notley, and was taken in such favour by the captain of the band that he is half a captain himself; and many is the time he has ridden through our village, robbing his old neighbours, and doing more harm in a night than months of hard work will put right; and often when I have chanced to meet him he has given me a look that has frozen the blood in my veins. I have always lived in fear of him all my life; but I was never in such peril before today."

"Peril enough, in all sooth," said the traveller. "How came it, pretty maiden, that you chanced to be all alone in the wood so near to the haunts of the robbers?"

"Nay, I was far enough away from their regular haunts. I had but come a short cut through the wood to see a sick neighbour, and I tarried beside her longer than I well knew. I will never do the like again, but I have been used from childhood to roam these forest paths unharmed. The wood is thick, and if I hear the sound of horse or man I always slip aside and hide myself. But today, methinks, they must have tracked me and were lying in wait; for the wood was silent as the church till I reached the clearing, and then the whole four sprang up from behind the pile of felled trees and set upon me. Had you not been at hand, by good providence; I should ere this have been their helpless captive;" and again the girl shuddered strongly.

By this time the trees were growing somewhat thinner, and lights began to twinkle here and there, showing that some village was nigh at hand. A bell for vespers began to ring forth, and the traveller was glad enough to think his toilsome journey nearly at an end. Hardy as he was, and well inured to fatigues and hardship of all kinds, he was growing exhausted from his day's travel and his sharp fighting. He was wounded, too, and although there was no great effusion of blood, his hurt was becoming painful, and his left arm, which was undoubtedly broken, required some skilled attention.

"Is it here that you live, fair maid?" he asked. "I know not how you are named; but I gather that you are directing our course to your own home."

"My name is Joan Devenish," she answered, "and the lights you see yonder are those of Much Waltham, and it is our church bell that you hear ringing out so sweetly. My father's farm is a mile beyond. But I beseech you ride thither with me. My mother would be ill pleased did I not bring home the gallant stranger who had saved me from my foes. And Figeon's will be proud to shelter such a guest."

"I give you humble thanks, Mistress Joan, and gladly would I find so hospitable a shelter. I am but a poor traveller, however, roaming the world in search of the fame and fortune that come not. I am one of those who have ever followed the failing fortunes of the Red Rose of Lancaster, and sorry enough has often been my plight. But if rumour speaks true, and the great Earl of Warwick has placed King Henry once again on his throne, then perchance I may retrieve the fallen fortunes of my house. My father and brothers laid down their lives for his cause; his foes took possession of our fair lands, and I was turned adrift on the wide world. But tell me, ere we journey farther, which Rose you and your house favour; for I would not bring trouble upon any, and my roving life has taught me that the House of Lancaster has many bitter foes."

"O sir, be not afraid," answered Joan eagerly; "we country folk are quiet and peaceable, and care little who wears the crown, so as we may till our land in peace, and be relieved from the hordes of robbers and disbanded soldiers who have swarmed the country so long. We have called ourselves Yorkists these past years, since King Edward has been reigning; but I trow if what men say is true, and he has fled the country without striking a blow for his crown, and the great earl has placed King Henry on the throne again, that we shall welcome him back. I know little of the great matters of the day. My father bids me not trouble my head over things too hard for me. I tend the poultry and the young calves, and let the question of kings alone."

The traveller smiled at this; but his companion was evidently something of a talker, and endued with her full share of feminine curiosity.

"I would gladly know your name, fair sir," she said shyly, "for I shall have to present you to my good father ere long."

"My name is Paul Stukely," he answered. "I am the youngest and only surviving son of one of King Henry's knights and loyal adherents. My parents are both dead, and I have long been alone in the world. I have little to call my own save my good horse and trusty weapons. But I sometimes hope that there may be better days in store, if the rightful king gets back his own again."

At that moment the travellers were passing by the village forge, and a bright gleam of light streamed across their path, revealing to a brawny young fellow at the door the weary horse and its double burden. He came one step nearer, and exclaimed:

"Why, Joan, what means this? You riding pillion fashion with a stranger! What, in the name of all the saints, has befallen you?"

Sultan had paused of his own accord at the forge, and Joan was eagerly telling her story to a little crowd of listeners, and making so much capital out of the heroism of her gallant rescuer that all eyes were turned upon the battered stranger; and whilst deep curses went up from the lips of many of the men as they heard of the last attempt of the Black Robbers upon one of their own village maidens, equal meed of praise and thanks was showered upon Paul, who leaned over his saddlebow in an attitude that bespoke exhaustion, though he answered all questions, and thanked the good people for their kindly reception of him, whilst trying to make light of his own prowess, and to give the credit of their final escape to Joan, to whom, indeed, it was due.

But the elder smith, John Ives, pushed his way through the little group round the black horse, and scattered them right and left.

"Good neighbours," he said, "can you not see that this gentleman is weary and wounded, and that his good horse is like to drop as he stands?

"Go to, Will. Lift down the maid, and lead her yourself up to Figeon's. I will conduct the gentleman thither, and tend his hurts myself.

"For, good sir, I know as much about broken bones as any leech in the countryside; and if you will but place yourself in my hands, I'll warrant you a sound man again before another moon has run her course. 'Tis a farrier's trade to be a bit of a surgeon; and the Iveses have been farriers in Much Waltham longer than any can mind.

"On then, good horse. 'Tis but a short mile farther; and a good stable and a soft bed, and as much fodder as you can eat, you will find at Figeon's Farm."

Paul was glad enough to have matters thus settled for him; and even Sultan seemed to understand the promise made him, for he pricked up his ears, dropped his nose for a moment into the kindly hand of the smith, and with the guiding hand upon his rein stepped briskly forward up the dark rough lane, through the thick belt of trees on either side. For in the days of which I write the great forest of Epping extended almost all over the county of Essex, the villages were scarcely more than small clearings in the vast wood, and only round the farms themselves were there any real fields worth calling by the name.

Will and Joan tripped on ahead more rapidly than Sultan or his master cared to go. Paul did not trouble himself any longer about the road he was traversing, leaving himself entirely in the kindly care of the smith. He even dozed a little in the saddle as the horse picked his way steadily through the darkness, and was only fully roused up again by the sight of lanterns dancing, as it seemed, over the ground, by the sound of rough yet pleasant voices, and the glimmer of steadier light through the latticed windows of some building near at hand. The next minute he was before the hospitable door of the old farmhouse.

A ruddy blaze streamed out through that open door. Friendly hands assisted him to alight, and guided him to a rude oak settle placed within the deep inglenook, which was almost like a small inner chamber of the wide farm kitchen. Some hot, steaming drink was held to his lips; and when he had drunk, the mist seemed to clear away from his eyes, and he saw that he was the centre of quite a group of simple rustics; whilst the pretty, dark-eyed Joan, in her gown of blue serge, with its big sleeves of white cloth, was eagerly watching him, all the time pouring out her story, which everybody appeared to wish to hear again and again.

"Just to think of it!" cried a burly man, whose dress bespoke him a farmer no less than his ruddy cheeks and horny hands. "Would that I had been there! He should not then have escaped with his life.

"Child, why didst thou not stab him to the heart as he lay?"

"Well has he been called Devil's Own by his former comrades and playfellows. A defenceless girl—my daughter! By good St. Anthony, if he crosses my path again it shall be for the last time. I will—"

"Hush, I pray you, good husband," said his wife more gently, though from the way in which she clasped her daughter to her breast it was plain she had been deeply moved by the story of her peril. "Remember what the Scriptures say: 'Thou shalt not kill,' 'Vengeance is mine,' and many like passages—"

But the woman stopped suddenly short, silenced by the grip of her husband's hand upon her arm. A quick look was exchanged between them, and she lapsed into silence.

The farmer glanced round him, and dismissed the serving wenches and labourers who had gathered round to their own quarters, and indeed in many cases to their beds; for early hours were all the fashion in those days. The farmer's wife beckoned her daughter, and went to prepare for the lodging of their guest; and before very long Paul found himself in a bed which, however rude according to our notions, was luxury itself to the weary traveller.

The smith soon saw to his hurts, pronounced them only trifling, and bound them up as cleverly as a leech would have done. Indeed, he was the regular doctor for most kinds of hurts, and could practise the rude surgery of the day with as much success as a more qualified man.

Evelyn Everett-Green

Paul had been weary enough half-an-hour before, but the good food he had taken and the hot spiced wine had effectually aroused him. He was very tough and well seasoned, and although glad enough to lie still in bed, was not particularly disposed for sleep; and when the smith was preparing to depart, he begged him to stay a while longer, and tell him something about the place and about the people he had come amongst. The worthy man was ready enough to chat, though he had little notion of imparting information. Still, he answered questions with frankness, and Paul was able to pick up a good deal of gossip as to public opinion in those parts and the feeling of the people round.

But what he heard did not give him pleasure. He had been in the north when he had heard of Warwick's sudden desertion of the Yorkist cause, and before he had been able to reach London he had heard the glad news that Henry of Lancaster was again on the throne, placed there by the power of the King Maker, who had dethroned him but a few years back. Glad as Paul was, he yet wished that any other hand had been the one to place the crown upon the gentle monarch's head. He could not but distrust Warwick, and he was eager to learn the feeling of the country, and to know whether or not the people welcomed back the sovereign so long a captive.

But in this place, at least, it seemed as if there was no pleasure in Henry's restoration. The smith shook his head, and said he had no faith in his keeping the crown now he had got it. It seemed as if the love borne by Londoners to Edward of York had extended as far as this remote village: the people had been enjoying again, under the later years of his reign, something of the blessings of peace, and were loath that their calm should be disturbed.

The feeling might not be patriotic, but it was natural, and Paul admitted with a sigh that the cause of the Red Rose was not likely to find favour here. A king who could fight and who could govern, and hold his kingdom against all comers, was more thought of than one who appeared a mere puppet in the hands of a designing noble or a strong-willed queen. The sudden desertion of Warwick from his banner had caused a momentary panic in Edward's army, and the king had fled with his followers beyond the sea; but, as the hardy smith remarked with a grim smile, he would not be long in coming back to claim his kingdom. And if the country were again to be plunged into the horrors of civil war, it would be better for the whole brood of Lancaster to seek exile or death.

Paul had not energy to argue for his cause, and fell asleep with these sinister words ringing in his ears.

Evelyn Everett-Green

CHAPTER 2

A HOSPITABLE SHELTER

Figeon's Farm (the true spelling of the name should be Fitz-John's, but nobody ever thought of calling it so) was a prosperous and pleasant place enough. It had been in the hands of Devenishes ever since the Norman conquest—so at least the common belief went—and there was no tradition of the house or lands having been in other hands than those of the present family.

When Paul Stukely awoke from the deep sleep of exhaustion into which he had fallen even while the worthy smith had been talking to him overnight, his ears were assailed by the peaceful and comfortable sounds inseparable from farm-house life and occupation. He heard the cackling of hens, the grunting of pigs, and the rough voices of the hinds as they got the horses out of the sheds, and prepared to commence the labours of the day with harrow or plough. These sounds were familiar enough to Paul; they seemed to carry him back to the days of his childhood, and he lay for several minutes in a state between sleeping and waking, dreamily wondering if the strange events of the past year were all a dream, and if he should wake by-and-by to find himself a child once more, in his little bed in the old home, and receive his mother's kiss as his morning's greeting.

But soon this sweet illusion faded, and the young man sat up in bed and looked quickly round him, trying to recollect where he was and what had brought him here. During the last two years, in which he had been forced to lead the roving life of an adventurer—common enough in those days, and by no means entirely distasteful to one of his temperament and training—he had slept in many strange places, and had known quarters far ruder than the unceiled, raftered room of the gabled farm.

In time it all came back to him—the attack upon the helpless girl in the wood, his own successful defence, and the journey to the farmhouse in the gathering darkness. Paul gave himself a shake to see how he felt, and decided that although stiff and bruised, and crippled in the left arm, he might yet make shift to rise and dress himself. He saw his clothes all laid out in readiness for him, and it was plain that some good friend had sat up far into the night brushing and mending them; for they had been in somewhat sorry plight after his adventure of yesterday, and now they were fresh and clean and almost smart looking, as they had not been for many a long day before.

As Paul was slowly dressing, he was suddenly aware of the sound of a woman's voice speaking or reading—he fancied from its monotonous cadence that it must be the latter—in some room that could not be far away from his own chamber. In those days such an accomplishment as reading was not at all common to the inhabitants of a farm, and Paul stood still in surprise to listen.

Yes, there was no mistaking it, there was certainly somebody—some woman—reading aloud in a chamber hard by. Presently the cadence of the voice changed, and Paul was certain that the reading had changed to prayer; but not the pattering Paternosters or Ave Marias with which he was

Evelyn Everett-Green

familiar enough. This style of prayer was quite different from that; and the young man, after listening for a few moments with bated breath, exclaimed to himself, in accents of surprise and some dismay:

"Lollards, in good sooth! By the mass, I must have stumbled into a nest of heresy;" and he crossed himself devoutly, as if to shield himself from the evil of contamination.

Paul had been born and bred a Papist, as indeed was the case with most of his countrymen in those days. The House of Lancaster was deeply attached to the faith as they found it, and Henry the Sixth had burned many a heretic at Smithfield; for he was at once a saint and a fanatic—a very common combination then, hard enough as it seems now to bracket the two qualities together—and led in all things by his ghostly advisers.

But the leaven of the new doctrines was silently working throughout the length and breadth of the land in spite of all repressive measures, and King Edward the Fourth, either from policy or indifference, had done little or nothing to check its spread. London—the place of all others which was ever loyal to him—was a perfect hotbed of heresy (in the language of the priests), and that alone was enough to deter the Yorkist monarch from stirring up strife and bringing down upon his head the enmity of the powerful city which served him so well. Now that the meek Henry wore the crown again—if indeed he did wear it—the Lollards might well tremble for their liberties and lives.

As for Paul, he had seen and heard little of the new religion, as he called it, and looked upon it as a terrible and deadly sin. At the same time, he had knocked about the world enough to have won a larger toleration for all sorts and conditions of men than he would have done had he remained master of the ancestral estates at home; and after a momentary thrill of dismay and repulsion, he decided to take no notice of what he had inadvertently overheard.

These people had been kind and friendly. If they desired him to remain a short time beneath their roof until his wounds were healed, he saw no particular reason against doing so. A spell of rest and quiet would suit him and Sultan very well, and with their private beliefs he had no concern; the less he knew of them the better.

So he finished his toilet, whistling a gay tune to drown the sound of the unauthorized prayer nigh at hand; and when he had finished he opened his door, and made his way down the narrow, winding stairs, into the great kitchen he had entered the previous evening.

The big place looked cheerful enough this bright morning: the door standing wide open to the October sunlight—the huge fire of logs crackling and blazing on the wide hearth and roaring up the vast open chimney—the rude metal and wooden utensils as clean as scrubbing could make them— and the brick floor clean enough to eat off, as the saying goes. And this cleanliness was not so common in those days of partial civilization as it is now: there were farmhouses enough and to spare in the England of that day where men and animals herded together amid filth that we should hardly condemn pigs to in this enlightened age. Wherefore Paul was both pleased and surprised by all he saw, and his dim misgivings fled away promptly.

In the wide inglenook before the oak settle a small table had been drawn up, and upon this table stood one wooden platter, and some homely viands sufficiently tempting to a hungry man, and a huge joram of home-brewed ale. Paul did not doubt for a moment that this was his own breakfast thus

Evelyn Everett-Green

temptingly spread for him; and he was fully disposed to do it ample justice, for he had eaten little during the past four-and-twenty hours, and had ridden far and done some good hard fighting to boot. But he did not like to sit down uninvited, and as he stood warming his hands at the pleasant blaze, there tripped into the room the girl he had last clearly seen, gun in hand, in the forest, and she greeted him with the prettiest smile and blush.

"Good morrow, fair sir. I am pleased indeed to see you thus afoot, and hope you feel little the worse for your brave encounter yesterday. We know not how to thank you; in truth, I scarce slept all last night, thinking what my fate must have been but for your timely rescue. But I pray you be seated, and try this pie of mother's own making, with a slice of home-cured ham (father is a great rearer of pigs; and the brothers of Leighs Priory, who know what good living is, always come to him for his primest bacon and ham). You look as if you needed a good meal, for your face is but wan this morning. Mother scarce looked to see you on your feet so soon."

Paul laughed as he sat himself down to the hospi table board.

"Nay, I scarce feel any ill effects from the knocks I got. A rover like myself is tough and wiry, or should be. I fear this arm may not be serviceable for a few weeks to come, but—"

"But if you will do us the pleasure to make this poor house your home until such time as you can go forth a sound man, you will be giving us great honour and pleasure; for I think that if harm had befallen our dear and only daughter, her father's heart would have broken, and her mother's hairs have gone down with sorrow to the grave."

It was a fresh voice that spoke these words, and Paul rose

instinctively to his feet as he found himself face to face with his hostess.

Mistress Devenish, as she was commonly called, was no ordinary buxom, loud-tongued farmer's wife, but a slight, small woman, of rather insignificant aspect, unless the expression of the face was taken into account. Then indeed might be seen a refinement and intellect seldom found in persons of her class in those rough and uncultured times. Paul, who was a shrewd observer, detected at once that this was no ordinary woman before him, and saw from whom Joan had inherited her graceful, refined bearing and sweet, low-toned voice. She was a much taller and finer woman than her mother had ever been, for she had something of her father's strength and stature; but for all that she owed much of her charm to her mother, and plainly regarded her with true filial devotion.

"I thank you heartily," answered Paul, as he held out his hand in greeting. "I should be glad enough to rest, for a few days at least, in such pleasant quarters; but I must not let myself become a burden to you because that I have had the honour of rendering a trifling service to fair Mistress Joan here."

"Nay, sir, it was no trifling service you did her; it was such service as must ever cause a mother's heart to swell with thankful joy. What would have become of the maid carried off by that evil man to his own secret haunts I dare not even think. Had they slain her before her parents' eyes, it would have been less terrible than to know her utterly at their mercy."

"Ay, indeed it would," cried the girl, with dilating eyes. "Ah, fair sir, you know not what monsters these terrible robbers can be. Oh, I pray you go not forth again until you can go a hale and sound man; for you have incurred by your act of yesterday the fury of one who never forgives, and who is as cunning as he is cruel. He may set his spies upon you; and dog your steps if you leave this place; and if you were to be overcome by them and carried off to their cave in the forest, some terrible and cruel death would surely await you there. For they truly call him Devil's Own—so crafty, so bloodthirsty, so full of malice and revenge has he ever shown himself."

The girl's cheek paled as she spoke; but Paul smiled at her fears. Not that he was altogether foolhardy, or disposed to despise warnings thus given him; but his life had taught him a certain hardihood and contempt of danger, and he and his good horse had proved match enough for formidable antagonists before now.

"I thank you for your kind thought for me, and I will use all prudence when I stir from the shelter of this hospitable roof. But my next journey will be to London, and there, methinks, shall I find more of law and order. It is a sad state of things when not forty miles from the king's own city bands of robbers abound and flourish, making honest folks tremble for their lives and liberties."

"You speak truly; young sir," answered Mistress Devenish, who had now sat down to her spinning wheel in the inglenook, whilst her daughter still hovered about restlessly, and waited assiduously upon their disabled guest. "And had King Edward but kept his throne, I verily believe he would have put down with a strong hand these same marauders who devastate the country more than war itself. Things were beginning to improve after the long and disastrous civil strife, and we fondly told ourselves that the worst was over, and that the distracted country would taste something of the blessings of peace again. But since that haughty earl men call the King Maker has gone to France to make his peace with the Lancastrian queen, and has returned to place her husband (poor man, it is no fault of his that he cannot sway the sceptre, but can only submit to the dictates of others) on England's throne, we shall again be plunged, I know it well, in bloody and terrible strife. The lion-hearted Edward will never resign his rights without a struggle. He will return and collect an army, and the cruel bloodshed will recommence. This bloodless victory will not last. God alone knows how the struggle will end. We know but too well that misery and desolation will be the fate of the country until the matter is finally settled one way or the other; and when will that be?"

Paul listened in grave silence to these words, so foreign to his own hopes and the confident expressions he had heard from time to time uttered by hot partisans of the Red Rose. He had hoped to find the whole country rejoicing in the restoration of the gentle monarch, whom he loved with the ardour of a generous and impetuous temperament. But these simple folks, rustic and unlettered though they were, managed somehow to throw a shadow over his spirit by their grave and doubting words.

He realized that King Henry would have a hard struggle ere the whole of England owned his sway. Edward was yet the king in many a part of the realm. He was more respected and beloved than the feeble, monk-ridden monarch he had deposed; and if it came to be a question of abstract right, none could dispute the superiority of the claim of the House of York. Edward was the descendant of the elder branch of the family of Edward the Third. It was only the politic reign of the fourth Henry, and the brilliant reign of the fifth, which had given to the House of Lancaster its kingly title. Men would probably never have thought of disputing the sixth Henry's sway had he held the sceptre firmly and played the part of king, to any purpose. But his health and temperament were alike feeble: he inherited the fatal malady of his grandsire of France, and was subject to fits of mental illness which made him utterly helpless and supine. His strong-minded queen was detested by the nobles and unpopular with the mass of the people, whilst the ambition of the powerful barons and peers had made civil strife an easy and popular thing.

There was no great issue at stake in these disastrous wars; no burning question was settled by the victory of either side; no great principle or national interest was involved. It was little more in reality than the struggle for supremacy and place amongst the overbearing and ambitious nobles; hence the ease and readiness with which they changed sides on every imaginable pretext, and the hopeless character of the struggle, which ruined and exhausted the country without vindicating one moral or national principle.

But Paul Stukely, at twenty years of age, was not likely to take this dispassionate view of the case. His whole heart was in the cause of the Red Rose, and he could scarce listen to these quiet but telling words without breaking out into ardent defence of the cause he had at heart.

"But listen, good mistress," he exclaimed eagerly, when she had ceased to speak: "there are better days dawning for the land than they have seen either beneath the rule of the gentle Henry or the bold but licentious Edward. His blessed majesty has no love for the office of king, and his long captivity has further weakened his health and increased his love for retirement. You speak truly when you doubt if he will ever rule this turbulent nation, so long torn with strife and divided into faction. But think—he need not sway the sceptre which has proved too heavy for his hands. He has a son—a fair and gallant prince—worthy of the royal name of Edward which he bears. Men say that it will not be the feeble father who will restore order to the country and bring peace again to its shores, but that the task will be intrusted to the youthful Edward, who in his person combines the graces of his stately mother and the warlike prowess of his great ancestor whose cognizance he bears. Trust me, good people, if you love not Henry you will love Henry's son; and will it not be better to be ruled by him than by that other Edward of York, the usurper, who, though I verily believe he can be a lion in battle, yet spends his days, when not in arms, in lolling in idleness and luxury amid his fine court beauties, and beseems himself rather as a woman than a man? I would fain serve a spotless prince, such as our noble Prince of Wales is known to be, than one whose life is stained by the debaucheries of a luxurious court, and gluttony such as it is a marvel even to hear of."

Joan's eyes lighted, as the youth spoke with all the ardour of a young and vivid imagination and a generous and undoubting love. Even the grave-faced woman at the spinning wheel smiled to herself, and though she heaved a little sigh, she answered gently enough:

"Ay, young sir, if that could be! If we could be ruled by one who was brave, and stainless, and wise, and just, then England might count itself a happy land indeed; but I have lived through troublous times, and I have lost hope in such a speedy and happy conclusion to the matter. But we shall see—we shall see."

"We have all favoured King Edward's cause here, as I told you yesterday," said Joan; "for we seemed better off under his rule than in the days before, when we were distracted by the war. But tell us of this prince—the Prince of Wales, as you call him. Would he be able to rule us wisely and well? Has he a strong arm and a kind heart? And does he think for himself? or do the monks or the queen direct him in all matters? Have you ever seen him? Do you know what he is like?"

Evelyn Everett-Green

"I have not seen him since he was a child and I a child, too," answered Paul, his face lighting at the recollection of the little prince of his dreams, which had never faded or grown dim. "In sooth, he was the noblest, kingliest child the sun ever shone on. And men say he has grown up to fulfil all the promise of his youth. He is solemnly betrothed, so they say, to the Lady Anne, the daughter of the proud Earl of Warwick, and it is into his hands that the real government of the country will be intrusted.

"Oh, you would love him if you could see him—I am sure of that. I would he could come himself now, for the hearts of the nation would surely go out to him. Shall I tell you a story of him when he was a child—when we were children together? You will see how sweet and lovable he was even then, and I warrant that he has not changed now."

Joan answered eagerly in the affirmative, and Paul told of his adventure with the little prince in the forest hard by Lichfield; and mother and daughter as they heard the tale exchanged glances, as if it was not the first time they had heard something of the kind. He had hardly finished the narrative before Joan broke eagerly in:

"O sir, was it in truth you that balked the robbers of their prey? I pray you never speak of this to any in these parts, for truly it might cost you your life. You have heard us speak of the Black Notley robbers, whose lawless band our neighbour joined—the one who tried yesterday to get me into his clutches? Well, this same story that you have told to us he has heard a dozen times from his chief—the chief of all the band—Fire Eater, as he is called in their fierce language. It was he and his followers who hung upon the royal party all those long years ago, and he who carried you off in mistake for the Prince of Wales. He has often been heard to swear terribly over that great disappointment, and regret that he did not run his sword through the body of the daring boy who had outwitted him. If he were to hear of your being here, he would move heaven and earth to obtain your capture or death.

"O sir, be advised, you are in more peril than you know. Go not forth from the shelter of these doors till you can do so a sound man, and then make hasty and swift flight for London, where perchance you may be safe. These terrible robbers are not to be smiled at; they are cunning and cruel and crafty beyond belief. I shiver even for myself whenever I think of that terrible Simon Dowsett, whom they call Devil's Own."

Paul was not a little surprised to hear that his childish exploit had been heard of here, and that the robber chief he had outwitted was the real leader of the band some members of which he had slain the previous day. He could not disguise from himself that he might on this account be placed in a position of some danger. The man whose villainous scheme he had frustrated would undoubtedly be his deadly enemy, and it was possible that if his name became known in the place, it would draw upon him the vengeance of the whole band. True, the robber chieftain might have forgotten the name of the child who had been carried off by him in mistake for the Prince of Wales; but Paul remembered how he had called it out when appealing to his friend the farmer for help, and it was possible that it might be remembered against him. Certainly, in his present crippled state, it seemed advisable to remain in hiding at the farm, as he was so hospitably pressed to do; and after a short debate with himself upon his position, he gratefully consented to do so.

"That is right, that is right," cried the farmer, when he came in at midday for the dinner that family and servants all shared together; and presently, when the meal was over, and the women had retired to wash up the platters in an adjoining

Evelyn Everett-Green

room, whilst the labourers had started forth for their labours, the master drew his guest into the warm inglenook again, and said to him in a low voice:

"I'll be right glad to have a good Lancastrian abiding beneath my roof for awhile. The good brothers of Leighs are our best customers, and one or another of them is always coming across on some errand, and 'twill do us no harm in their eyes to find a follower of King Henry under our roof. I know not how it is, but of late they have been somewhat changed toward us;" and the farmer looked uneasily round, as if hardly knowing who might be listening. "We go to mass as regular as any; and my little girl there has worked a robe for the reverend prior himself as cost me a pretty penny in materials, and half blinded her pretty eyes, she sat at it so close. They have no need to look askance at us; but there, there, I suppose they have had a deal of trouble with the heretic books and such like as have been getting about the country of late. They say they found a Wycliffe's Bible hidden under the hearth stone of a poor woman's cottage in Little Waltham, nigh at hand here; and if King Henry had been on the throne, she might have been sent up to Smithfield to be burned, as an example and warning to others. But King Edward was on the throne then, and he cares not to burn his subjects for heresy—God bless him for that! But if King Henry is coming back to reign, it behoves all good persons to be careful and walk warily. So, young sir, if you can speak a good word for us to the holy brothers, I will thank you with all my heart. It's a bad thing when they get the notion that a house is corrupted by heresy."

The palpable uneasiness of the farmer betrayed to Paul full well that he was very much afraid of the orthodoxy of his wife, and it was not impossible that he himself might not be secretly favouring the new religion whilst conforming outwardly in all things. Such cases were by no means rare, and this village appeared Yorkist enough in its sentiments to suggest suspicions as to its orthodoxy.

But Paul was young and impressionable and generous; he liked these good folks, and knew nothing whatever to their discredit. He was sure that, whatever they might privately believe, they were good and trustworthy folks, and he gave his word to do all that he could, if chance offered, with an emphasis that won him the hearty thanks of the farmer.

Nor was the chance very long in coming: for only on the afternoon of the next day a portly monk jogged up to the farm on his sleek palfrey; and Paul, who was seated near to the door, rose and bent his knee, asking the customary blessing; after which the monk dismounted, and made his way into the kitchen to give some order to the good mistress of the house.

The monks of those days were regular gossips, and loved a chat, as they sat in the chimney corner enjoying a cup of the best wine the house afforded, or a substantial meal of the choicest products of the larder. Brother Lawrence was no exception to this rule; and the farmer's wife bestirred herself to get him everything he could fancy, whilst he sat and questioned Paul as to his history and the adventure which had brought him to this homestead. Very much did he enjoy hearing of the discomfiture of the robbers, and laughed quite merrily to think how they had been overcome by the handsome stripling before him.

Presently, when Mistress Devenish had gone away to make some inquiries respecting the flitches of bacon required for the Priory, Brother Lawrence beckoned Paul somewhat nearer, and said, in a low voice, in his ear:

"Be in no haste to depart from hence, my son. It may be that

Evelyn Everett-Green

there is work for you here for the Holy Church. It is whispered by one and another that yon good woman, as I would fain believe her to be, is somewhat tainted with the damnable heresy they call Lollardism, and that she has in her possession one of those Bibles which that arch-heretic Wycliffe translated into the vulgar tongue for the undoing of the unlearned, who think that they can thus judge for themselves on matters too high for them. You, my son, as a true son of the Church, may do us great service by keeping open both ears and eyes, and telling if you see or hear ought amiss. I would fain learn that no such evil is done among these good folks; but if it be that the leaven is working, it will be your duty to tell us thereof, and we will see if the evil may not be stamped out ere it has spread to others, or much corrupted even them that are tainted. We trust that the days are dawning now when Holy Church will have her ancient powers restored, and will be able to deal with heretics even as they merit. But however that may be, be it your work to watch and listen with all the powers you have. I trust that there will be nought you will hear save what is to the credit of these worthy folks."

Paul secretly in his heart vowed that no syllable which should hurt his hosts should ever pass his lips; but he bent his head with due reverence before the monk, who smiled and nodded cheerily to him before he went his way. It seemed strange that so jovial and kindly a man should so lightly speak of burning to death fellow creatures whom he had regarded for years with kindly goodwill. But there were strange anomalies in those days, even as there are in our own, and Paul saw nothing strange in this, nor in his own conduct, which made him appear submissive to the dictates of the Holy Church, as he ever called her in his thoughts, whilst all the time he was resolved neither to hear nor to see any of the things which would, if made known, injure his hosts in the eyes of the spiritual authorities. The very teaching of those spiritual pastors inculcated a certain amount of deceit and double dealing. What wonder if the weapon so freely used by themselves sometimes turned its double edge against them in its turn?

Paul accompanied the monk to the gate which led to the so-called road by which Figeon's was approached. It was nothing but a rude cart track; and although well-tilled fields lay on one side of this track, the forest lay upon the other, stretching away black and dim into immeasurable distance.

Paul lingered a little while beside the gate, watching the friar descend the sloping path; and he might have remained longer than he knew, for he was aroused from his day dream by the growl of one of the farm dogs, who stood at his side. Looking quickly round him, he fancied he detected amid the shadows of the trees across the road a dark figure almost concealed behind a solid trunk, the face alone visible—a dark, saturnine face, with a pair of eyes that gleamed like those of some wild beast.

The moment those eyes met Paul's the head was withdrawn, and the youth stood asking himself if it were not all a dream; but if it had been one, it was remarkably clear and vivid, and he walked to the house with a look of deep thought upon his face.

Evelyn Everett-Green

CHAPTER 3

A STRANGE ENCOUNTER

"Let me go," said Paul; "I should like the walk through the wood. I am quite strong again now, and I am weary of doing nothing from morning to night."

"Well, I don't know why you should not if it pleases your fancy," said the farmer. "You will be welcome at the Priory, as all guests are who come with news for the holy brothers from the world without. 'Tis less than four miles away, and you have got the use of your legs. Go, and welcome, if you will."

"I would go with you, were I not bound to go to Chelmsford myself," quoth Jack, the farmer's ruddy-faced son, of whom mention has not yet been made.

Paul had indeed seen but little of him so far, as his time was mainly spent in the fields, and he had been absent from home on his first arrival there, buying some fat sheep to be killed and salted down for consumption in the winter.

"I like well enough a visit to the Priory. There is always good cheer there enough and to spare. They know what good living means, those holy men. If all other trades failed, I would not mind turning friar myself."

"Nay, brother, jest not upon the holy men," quoth his sister in a tone of gentle reproof. Then turning to Paul, she added, with something of pleading in her tones, "But, sir, why peril yourself by venturing into the forest alone? You have still but the use of one arm, and were the robbers to be on the watch for you, you would fall an easy prey into their hands."

But Paul laughed, as also did Jack.

"I trow the robbers have something else to do than to play the spy continually on me and my movements," he said. "They cannot always be on the watch, and the wood is dark and full of hiding places. Were I to hear the sound of pursuit, I warrant me I could hide myself so that none should find me. I have done the like many a time before now. In this part of the country one must needs go into the forest if one is ever to leave the shelter of the house at all. Have no fear for me; I will take care not to run into danger."

Joan looked as if hardly satisfied, though she was unable to uphold her case by argument; for it was very true that if their guest was to be anything but a close prisoner, he must adventure himself from time to time in the forest. Jack, however, broke into one of his hearty laughs, as he looked at Paul, and said:

"Those same robbers are not such bad fellows, after all, as some of our good folks would make out. True, they help themselves to our goods from time to time; but they are capital company if you chance to fall upon their haunts, and they make you welcome. I've spent more than one night amongst them, and never a bit the worse. Men must live; and if the folks in authority will outlaw them, why, they must jog along then as best they may. I don't think they do more harm

Evelyn Everett-Green

than they can well help."

Mistress Devenish shook her head in silence over the rather wild talk of her son, but she said nothing. She was used to Jack's ways, and she was proud of his spirit, though afraid sometimes that it would lead him into trouble. She had noted of late that he had been unwontedly absent from home during the long evenings of the summer just gone by, and had wondered what took him off, for he seldom gave account of himself. She noted, too, that he spoke in a very different fashion from others of the robber band that was such a terror to the village folks. She did not know whether or not to put these two facts together as connected with each other; but she listened eagerly to all he said on the subject, trying to discover what might be the meaning of this strange leniency of opinion. "It is different for you, brother—they owe you no grudge," said Joan, with a slight shiver; whilst the farmer broke in roughly:

"Tut, tut, Jack! what mean you by trying to make common cause with the ruffians who would have carried your sister off as a prey of that graceless scamp well-called Devil's Own? I marvel to hear such words from you. You should know better."

"They are not all brutes like Devil's Own," muttered Jack in a low tone; but he did not speak aloud, for the fashion of the day forbade the young to argue with the old, or children to answer back when their parents spoke to them in reproof.

But Paul was still resolved that he would be the messenger to carry to the Priory that day the two fat capons the worthy mistress had in readiness for the prior's table. They had been bespoken some time, and could be no longer delayed. Paul was weary of an idle life, and eager to see something of the country in which he found himself. He was in comfortable quarters enough at the farm; but he was growing stronger each day, and was beginning to fret against the fetters which held him from straying far from the farm.

He did not much believe in the lasting anger of the robber band. He knew that those gentlemen would have other matters on hand than that of revenging themselves upon him for his frustration of their captain's design. He was content to rest yet awhile beneath the hospitable roof of the Figeons, so long as he knew that his presence there might be something of a protection and gain to its inmates; but he had no intention of being a prisoner. His young blood stirred within him, and he longed to be out in the free air of heaven again. His strength had all come back, and even the broken arm was mending so fast that he felt it would not be long before he should gain its full use again. The love of adventure, strong within him, made him fearless even of a second encounter with the robbers. He felt certain he could hold his own against one or two, and a whole band would never take him unawares. He should hear or see them in plenty of time to hide away in some tree or thicket. It was absurd to be chained within doors any longer.

Paul was looking now a very different object from the battered and way-worn traveller who had rescued Joan from the robbers. A couple of weeks' rest and good feeding had given a healthy glow to his cheek, had brightened his eye, and brought back the native boyishness and brightness to his face. He was stronger, gayer, blither than he had been since the never-to-be-forgotten day when he had closed his dead mother's eyes, and been obliged to fly for his life from his ancestral halls, ere the rapacious scions of the House of York fell upon him there, to take into their own possession all that should have been his. For his father and brothers lay in a bloody grave, killed in one of those many risings and insurrections scarce mentioned in history, whereby the

Evelyn Everett-Green

adherents of the Red Rose sought to disturb Edward's rule in England, and incite the people to bring back him they called their rightful king.

Those days had changed Paul, a mere lad of seventeen, into a grave and sad-faced man; but the impression had gradually worn somewhat faint during the three years in which he had been a wanderer and an outcast from his home. Of late it had seemed to him that his lost youth was returning, and certainly there was that in his bright glance and erect and noble bearing which won for him universal admiration and affection.

He was, in truth, a right goodly youth. His features were very fine, and the dark-gray eyes with their delicately-pencilled brows were full of fire and brilliance. The lips readily curved to a bright smile, though they could set themselves in lines of resolute determination when occasion demanded. The golden curls clustered round the noble head in classic fashion, but were not suffered to grow long enough to reach the shoulders, as in childhood's day; and the active, graceful, well-knit figure gave indication of great strength as well as of great agility.

Paul's dress, too, was improved since we saw him last; for one of the travelling peddlers or hawkers who roamed the country with their wares, and supplied the remote villages with the greater part of those articles not made at home, had recently visited Figeon's Farm, and Paul had been able to supply himself with a new and serviceable suit of clothes, in which his tall figure was set off to the best advantage.

It was made of crimson cloth and the best Spanish leather, and was cut after one of the most recent but least extravagant fashions of the day. Paul had been able to purchase it without difficulty, for he had by no means exhausted the funds he had in his possession, and the leather belt he wore next his person was still heavy with broad gold pieces.

Lady Stukely had seemed to have a prevision of coming trouble for her youngest-born son for many long years before the troubles actually came, and she had been making preparation for the same with the patience and completeness that only a mother's heart would have prompted. She had made with her own hands a stout leather belt, constructed of a number of small pouches, each one of which could contain a score of broad gold pieces. She knew full well that lands might be confiscated, valuables forfeited, houses taken in possession by foes, but the owner of the current gold of the land would never be utterly destitute; so for years before her death she bad been filling this ingeniously contrived belt, and had stored within its many receptacles gold enough to be a small fortune in itself. This belt had been in Paul's possession ever since the sad day when she had kissed him for the last time and had commended him to the care of Heaven. He had by no means yet exhausted its contents, for he had often won wages for himself by following one or another great noble in his private enterprises against some lawless retainer or an encroaching neighbour.

A little money went a long way in those days, when open house was kept by almost all the great of the land, and free quarters and food were always to be had at any monastery or abbey to which chance might guide the wanderer's feet. So Paul had not been forced to draw largely upon his own resources, and was a man of some substance still, although his compact little fortune was so well hidden away that none suspected its presence.

And now, his health restored, his strength renewed and his outer man refurbished in excellent style, Paul began to weary of the seclusion and monotony of the farm, and was eager to enjoy even the mild relaxation of a walk across to the brothers of the neighbouring Priory. The basket was soon packed, and was intrusted to his care; and off he set down the easy slope which led from Figeon's to Much Waltham, whistling gaily as he moved, and swinging his heavy burden with an ease that showed how little he made of it.

Will Ives, the blacksmith's son, was looking out from the rude forge as he passed, and came out to speak a friendly word to the fine young gentleman, as he now looked to rustic eyes. Honest Will's face had grown somewhat gloomy of late, though Paul did not know it, and he was suffering, if the truth must be told, from the keen pangs of jealousy. For he had long been courting Joan Devenish, and hoped to make her his wife before the year's end, and he fancied that she was disposed to his suit, although she had never given a direct reply to his rather clumsy but ardent wooing.

Of course it seemed to the young smith that every man in the world must be equally enamoured of his sweetheart, and he was terribly afraid that this fine young gentleman, with his handsome face and graceful figure, and pleasant voice and ways, would altogether cut him out with saucy Mistress Joan, who, it must be confessed, was fond of teasing her faithful swain, and driving him to the verge of distraction. So it showed Will's good-heartedness that he did not shun and dislike his rival, but rather, when he found him bent on an errand into the forest, offered to go with him part of the way, to make sure that all was safe.

"We haven't seen anything of the robbers round here lately, and they always give the Priory a wide berth, being half afraid of incurring the ban of Holy Church, though they care little about anything else. Anyway, I'll walk a part of the way with you, and carry the basket for a spell. Not but what you look brave and hearty again, in good faith."

Paul was ready enough for company, and Will soon got talking of his own private affairs, and presently it all came out—how he had loved Joan ever since they had been children together; how he had worked hard these past three years to save money to furbish up a little home for her; and how he was now building a snug little cottage under shelter of his father's larger one, so that he might have a little place for her all her own, seeing that she had been used to the space and comfort of the farm. To all this Paul listened with good-humoured interest, only wondering why Will's face kept so lugubrious, as if he were speaking of something which he had hoped for, but which could never be.

"You will have to look a little brighter when you come a-wooing," he said at length, "or Mistress Joan will be frightened to look at you. And why have you kept away so much these last days? She has been quite offended by it, I can tell you. It's always being said that you are sure to come today; and when the day goes by and you come not, she pouts and looks vexed, and casts about for all manner of reasons to account for it. You had better not be too slack, or you will offend her altogether."

Will's face brightened up marvellously.

"Then you think she cares?"

"Why, of course she does. She's forever talking of you and all you have done, and what a wonderful Will you are. When she sits at her wheel and chatters to me as I lounge by the fire, she is always telling of you and your sayings and doings. Why, man, did you not know that for yourself? Did you think all the love was on your side?"

"I daresay I was a fool," said Will, getting fiery red. "But I thought, perhaps, she would not care for a clumsy fellow like me after she had seen a gentleman like you. You saved her life, you know, and it seemed natural like that you should care for each other afterward. I know I'm nothing like you."

"No, indeed. I'm a mere wanderer—here today and gone tomorrow; a soldier and an outcast, who could never ask any woman to share his lot. My good sword is my bride. I follow a different mistress from you. I may never know rest or peace till the House of Lancaster is restored to its ancient rights. You need not fear me as a rival, good Will; for no thought of marriage has ever entered my head, and sometimes methinks it never will."

The smith's face was a study as he listened to these welcome words, and Paul laughed as he read the meaning of those changing expressions.

"Give me the basket, and get you gone to Figeon's, and make your peace with your offended lady," he said, laughing. "You are but a sorry wooer if you yield so soon to depression and despair. But I warrant she will forgive you this time; and if you will but plead your cause in good earnest, it may be that I shall yet have the pleasure of treading a measure at your wedding feast."

The blushing smith was easily persuaded to this course, and bade farewell to his companion in eager haste. He was clad only in his working apron, and his hands were grimy from his toil; but his open face was comely and honest enough to please the fancy of any maiden, and Paul thought to himself that Mistress Joan would scarce reject so stalwart a champion after the fright and the shock of the previous week but one. As Will Ives's wife she would be safer and better protected than as Farmer Devenish's unwedded daughter.

As for himself, thoughts of love and marriage had seldom

entered his mind, and had always been dismissed with a light laugh. As he had said to Will, he was wedded to a cause, to a resolute aim and object, and nothing nearer or dearer had ever yet intruded itself upon him to wean away his first love from the object upon which it had been so ardently bestowed. The little prince—as in his thoughts he still called him sometimes—was the object of his loving homage. King Henry was too little the man, and Queen Margaret too much, for either of them to fulfil his ideal or win the unquestioning love and loyalty of his heart; but in Edward, Prince of Wales, as he always called him, he had an object worthy of his admiration and worship.

Everything he heard about that princely boy seemed to agree with what he remembered of him in bygone years. He and not the gentle and half-imbecile king would be the real monarch of the realm; and who better fitted to reign than such a prince?

The kindly welcome he received at the Priory from Brother Lawrence and the prior himself was pleasant to one who had so long been a mere wanderer on the face of the earth. The beautiful medieval building, with its close-shorn turf and wide fish ponds, was a study in itself, and lay so peacefully brooding in the pale November sunshine, that it was hard to realize that the country might only too soon be shaken from end to end by the convulsions of civil war.

Paul was eagerly questioned as to what he knew of the feeling of the country, and he could not deny that there was great discontent in many minds at the thought of the return to power of the Lancastrian king. The monks and friars shook their heads, and admitted with a sigh that they feared the whole county of Essex was Yorkist to the core, and that it was the leaven of heretical opinions which was at the root of their rebellion against their lawful king. It was difficult to

Evelyn Everett-Green

believe that the warlike Edward would long remain an exile, content to deliver up a kingdom which had once been his without striking a single blow, especially when his own party was so powerful in the land.. London, a hotbed of Lollardism, would soon raise its voice in the call for Edward of York. The present hour was calm and bright, and Henry of Windsor wore his crown again; but the mutterings of the coming storm seemed already to be heard in the distance, and the brothers of the monastery did not blind their eyes to the fact that the wheel of fortune might still have strange turns in store.

"Wherefore we must walk warily, and not stir up strife," quoth the rubicund prior, who looked at once a benevolent and a strong-willed man. "We will pray for the restoration— the permanent restoration of the good king; but we must avoid stirring up the hearts of his subjects in such a way as will make them his foes.

"Young sir, what think you of your hosts at the farm? Are they quiet and well-disposed people, seeking in all things the good of the people, and giving due reverence to Holy Church?"

Paul answered eagerly in the affirmative. He had heard or seen nothing of a suspicious character of late, and had grown very fond of the kindly folks, who made him so welcome to the best of what they had. His reply was considered very satisfactory, and the prior dismissed him with his blessing; for Paul had no wish to be belated in the forest, and proposed to return immediately after the midday meal which he had shared with the brothers.

It was in somewhat thoughtful mood that he pursued his way through the woodland paths. Conversation about the burning questions of the day always left him with a feeling akin to depression. He longed for the restoration of the house he loved and served, but knew that a transitory triumph was not a true victory. There was still much to be done before Henry's seat upon the throne could be called secure; and what would be the result of the inevitable struggle of the next months?

He had unconsciously stopped still in deep thought as he asked himself this question, and was leaning in meditation against a great oak tree, when he suddenly became aware of a rapid tread approaching along the narrow track. It seemed as if some youth were advancing toward him, for he heard the clear whistle as of a boyish voice, and the springy tread seemed to denote youth and agility.

Although Paul was by no means afraid of a chance encounter in the forest, he was well aware that it was possible to be overreached and taken prisoner by some of the robbers, and that he was an object of special hatred to some amongst them. He decided, therefore, to act with caution; and as the spot in which he had halted was rather an open one, through which meandered a little brook, he resolved to slip silently into the thicket hard by, and watch from that place of security what manner of person it was advancing.

A moment later he had effectually concealed himself, and hardly had he done so before a figure came into view through the dim aisles of the wood.

The figure was that of a tall, slim, graceful youth of singularly winning aspect. His frame displayed that combination of strength, lightness, and agility which is the perfection of training, and his face was as full of beauty as his frame of activity and grace. The features were exceedingly noble, and the poise of the head upon the shoulders was almost princely in its unconscious majesty. The eyes were a deep blue gray,

Evelyn Everett-Green

and looked out upon the world as if their owner were born to rule. The hair was golden in hue, and clustered round the head in manly fashion, not in the flowing love locks that some in those days affected. The dress he wore was very simple, and somewhat faded, and in his cap a little silver swan was fastened, forming the only adornment on his person.

Paul, as he lay in his ambush, gazed and gazed as if fascinated upon the figure now standing stationary in the midst of the green space. Instinctively he felt for the little silver swan in his own cap, and looked to see if he had on by mistake the faded dress he had previously worn, so like the one he now gazed upon. For it seemed to him as though he saw his own double—or someone closely resembling himself—and his heart began to beat almost to suffocation; for had not this same experience been his before? and could there be another, a third youth in the realm, whose face and figure he had so accurately copied? Paul had not the royal mien of this wanderer—he had not even the same absolute beauty of feature or peculiar delicacy of colouring; but for all that the likeness was so striking that it was bewildering to him to see it, and the images and visions at once conjured up before his mind's eye were of a nature to excite him beyond the bounds of consecutive thought. Holding his breath, and still uncertain if he might not be dreaming, he fastened his eyes upon the apparition, and waited for what should happen.

The youth paused and looked round him, and then spoke aloud:

"Have I come on a fool's errand after all? Shall I ever accomplish my object? Methinks if I had but a trusty comrade at hand somewhat might be done; but I fear my poor Jacques never reached the land alive, and I had trusted to him to be my guide and counsellor in my quest. Alone I feel helpless—stranded—bewildered.

"Ha! what is that? Who comes this way?"

"Your faithful servant, gracious prince," cried Paul, springing out of his concealment and throwing himself at young Edward's feet. "My dear, dear lord, how come you here alone, unarmed, defenceless, in the midst of a hostile country? Methinks I do but dream; but yet the face, the voice—I cannot be mistaken. O sweet prince, did we not truly say that we should meet again? Do you remember me?"

"Remember you, good Paul? Of a truth I do, and that right well; and it is indeed a happy chance that has thrown you across my path this day. But Paul, on your life, on your loyalty as a subject, call me not prince again. It might cost me my life, and you yours.

"Hush! I will be obeyed, and I will explain in brief. I am here unknown to all. I stole away from my mother's side, even as I stole into the forest with you when we were but boys together. She thinks me with her sister, the Princess Yolande. But I had my own purpose in coming thus alone and disguised to our royal realm of England. They say my father reigns here once again. The crown has been placed upon his head by one I have almost the right now to call my father-in-law. But what rule has he, in truth, who reigns not in his people's hearts? What use to seek the empty glory of a golden crown, who wins not the priceless guerdon of a nation's love?

"Listen then, Paul. They tell me that in my hands will the kingly power soon be placed. If that is to be so, I would fain learn for myself the temper of my people. And this is not to be learned by Edward, Prince of Wales, seated in the midst of proud nobles at his father's court; but it may be learned by a humble wayfarer, who travels from place to place seeking information from whence it may truly be culled—namely,

Evelyn Everett-Green

from the artless sons of the soil, who speak not to please their listener but as their heart dictates.

"Paul, tell me I have done well—smile upon me again; for I am very lonely, and my heart sometimes sinks. But I love my people, and would be loved by them, only I needs must grow to know them first."

"O my lord," cried Paul enthusiastically, "how can they help loving you when they see you? But how come you alone, and in these wild woods, too, infested by fierce robber bands? It is not meet thus to peril your royal life."

The prince placed his hand smilingly on Paul's lips.

"Use not that word again," he said smilingly, yet with a certain imperiousness of manner that became him well. "I am thus solitary through the untoward accident that drowned the faithful follower who alone shared my design, and I knew not that I was in peril from these lawless men in one part of the realm more than the other. Paul, if I ever wield the kingly power, I will put down these bands of marauders with a strong hand. My peaceful subjects shall not go in terror of their liberties and lives. I would learn all their wrongs that I may right them. They shall know at last that a prince who loves them has been in their midst."

"And, my lord, if you are thus alone and unattended, take me with you on your travels. Did you not promise me long years ago that the day would come when we should roam the world together? and has not the time come now?"

"Why, verily I believe it has," cried Edward, with brightening eyes. "But, Paul, I have not asked you of yourself. Have you no other tie—no stronger claim? And how comes it that you are here, so far away from your home? I have asked not your history, though I have told mine own."

"Mine is soon told, sweet prince," said Paul. "I crave your pardon, but I know not how else to frame my speech."

Then in a few graphic words he sketched the history of himself and his kindred during those troubled years of civil strife and of Edward's reign; and young Edward listened with a sorrowful air and drooping mien, and heaved a deep sigh at the conclusion.

"Another faithful house ruined—another tale of woe for which it seems we unhappy princes are the cause. Nay, Paul, I know what you would say, brave loyal heart; but it lies heavy on my soul for all that. And having suffered thus, why tempt your fate anew by linking your fortunes with those of the hapless House of Lancaster? Why not—"

"My lord, break not my heart by rejecting my poor services," cried Paul, plunging anew into the tale of his longing and ambition to be one day called the servant of the Prince of Wales; and then as both were young, both ardent, hot-headed, and hopeful, all stern and sorrowful thoughts were laid aside, and the two youths began to plan with eager vehemence the future of adventure which lay before them.

"And first, Paul, this you must learn once and for all: I am prince no more, but Edward alone, Edward Stukely—for I will e'en borrow your good name—your younger brother, who seeks his fortune with you. I will pass as cousin here, where you are known, but elsewhere it shall be as brothers we will travel. This strange likeness will be my best safeguard, for none will doubt that we are close akin. Not as knight and squire, as once we thought, will we roam the world in search of adventure. This little realm of England will suffice us, and hand in hand as brothers will we go. But

Evelyn Everett-Green

methinks we shall surely meet as many strange adventures as in our dreams; and if I ever sit at last on England's throne, this journey of thine and mine will be for years the favourite theme of minstrels to sing in bower and hall."

CHAPTER 4

PAUL'S KINSMAN

"Kinsman—marry, a brother in very sooth!" cried the hospitable farmer, eying Paul's young companion with a glance of shrewd admiration and surprise; "and right welcome shall he be to such good cheer as my poor house can afford.

"And how found you your brother, fair youth?—for it can scarce have been chance that led you here. My guest spoke not of bringing you home when he started forth today."

"Nay, he knew it not himself," answered the prince, laughing merrily. "Nor is he my brother, good mine host: our kinship is a less close one than that, for all that we favour each other so well. He had no thought of the encounter when he started forth today, but kind fortune guided us to the meeting. As children we loved each other and played together, but for years we have not met. I am nought but a solitary wanderer, without friends or home. It has been a happy chance that has brought to me this trusty comrade and the welcome of this hospitable home."

There was something so attractive in the aspect and speech of the royal youth that all who heard him felt their hearts go

Evelyn Everett-Green

out to him, they knew not why. The farmer laid his horny hand on the lad's arm, and cried in his jovial way:

"All travellers, be they gentle or simple, are welcome at Figeon's Farm, and doubly so anyone who claims kinship with our guest and very good friend Paul Stukely. And you come at a good time, too, young sir; for we have a wedding feast in prospect, and we shall want all the blithe company we can assemble to make merry at it.

"Come, my wench; you need not run away. You are not ashamed of honest Will; and these gentlemen will doubtless honour our poor home by remaining our guests a while longer, that they may tread a measure at your marriage feast."

Paul looked smilingly at the blushing Joan, whose face was alight with happiness, and her father continued laughingly:

"Oh ay, they have made it up together this very day; and poor Will, who has been courting her these three years and more, cannot see what there is to wait for—no more can I. For my part, since that rascally Simon tried to carry off the girl, I have known no peace about her. Figeon's is a lonely place, and the young know not how to be cautious, and it's ill work for young blood to be cooped up ever between four walls. Down in the village, with neighbours about her, the wench will be safe enough, and Will's sturdy arm will be her best protection. Simon might think twice about assaulting a wedded woman to carry her away, when he would count a maid fair spoil, seeing that he ever claimed to be called a lover of hers. So all ways she will be safer wed, and I see no cause for them to wait."

And indeed in those unsettled and troubled times fathers were glad enough to get their daughters safely married at the first reasonable opportunity. Farmer Devenish had another reason in wishing Joan to leave her home. He was afraid that she might imbibe the views her mother had embraced, and which he and his son could not but give credence to, whilst they made no protest of having altered their old way of thinking. But he had always forbidden his wife to disturb Joan in her pious faith in the old religion. Such hard matters, he said, were not for young wenches; and the peril which menaced those who embraced the reformed doctrines was sufficiently terrible for the mother to be almost glad of the prohibition. It would be an awful thing for her if her daughter fell under the ban of the law, and was made to answer for her faith as some had been in so cruel a fashion before now.

So that there was no wish on the part of any at the old home to hinder her marriage, and as soon as the young people had come to an understanding with one another, their way was made perfectly plain by those in authority.

Joan looked shyly at Paul as he crossed the kitchen with some pleasant word of congratulation, and said:

"In faith, kind sir, I think we owe it all to you. Will tells me it was you who sent him hither today. He had got some foolish notion in his head which kept him away; but he said it was you who bid him take heart and try his luck."

"And very good luck he has had, it seems," answered Paul, laughing. "And so the marriage is to be next week?"

"My father and mother wish it so," answered the blushing Joan; "and my mother has long had all my household linen spun against the wedding day. I trust you will stay, and your kinsman also. Perchance you have never before seen a rustic wedding."

Evelyn Everett-Green

"Not for many years now," answered Paul, with a smile and a sigh; "and I would fain be a witness of yours, fair mistress. But I must ask my young companion there. We have linked our lives together for the nonce."

But young Edward was perfectly willing to be the farmer's guest for awhile. Nothing could better have fitted in with his own wishes than to have stayed in such unquestioned fashion beneath the roof of one of his humble subjects. At the supper table that night he won all hearts by the grace of his manners, the sweetness of his smiles, his ready courtesy to all, and the brilliant sallies that escaped his lips which set the whole table sometimes in a roar. He possessed that ready adaptability to circumstances which is often an attribute of the highest birth. The motherly heart of Mistress Devenish went out to him at once, and she would fain have known something of his history, and how it came that so fair and gentle a youth was wandering thus alone in the wide world.

Paul had told her all his story without the least reserve; but this kinsman of his was more reticent, and if asked a question, contrived to turn the edge off it without appearing to avoid giving a direct answer. But Mistress Devenish was acute enough to perceive that he did not intend to speak of his own past; and noting the unconscious deference paid by Paul to one whom seniority would have given him the right to dictate to and lead, she came to the conclusion that, kinsfolk or no, the newcomer was of a more exalted rank than his comrade, and that some romantic history attached to him, as it did only too often, to wanderers in those days. Her interest in him only deepened as she reached this conclusion, and she wished that she knew how to help the two lonely youths whose fates seemed now to be linked together.

Supper was in course, and the whole party assembled round the table, when a knock at the outer door, heralded by a great barking of dogs without, caused one of the men to start to his feet; whilst Joan turned red and pale, as she had had a trick of doing of late; and the farmer looked a trifle uneasy, as a man may do who is half afraid of some domestic visitation of an unpleasing kind.

But when the door was opened, brows cleared and anxious looks vanished; for the visitor was none other than the peddler of a few days back, who, contrary to custom, had paid a second visit to the village within a week of the first.

"Good even, good folks," he said, stepping in with his heavy bags, which he deposited with a grunt upon the floor. "You will wonder to see me so soon again, but I was turned from my course by the breaking down of the bridge at Terling, and so I thought I would tramp back the way I had come. Reaching the village at sundown, I heard the news of the wedding that is to be up here; and, thought I, surely where a wedding is to be the peddler is always welcome. So here I am, and I doubt not you will give me a night's shelter; and the pretty maid is welcome to turn over my packs at her leisure, whilst I take my ease in yon cozy inglenook."

The peddler was always a welcome guest in those days, and Peter was eagerly welcomed by all. He was speedily seated at the board, the best of everything heaped upon his trencher; whilst as he talked and ate at the same time, doing both with hearty goodwill, Joan and one of the serving wenches slipped away to the tempting packs and undid the strings, handling the wares thus exposed with tender care and delighted curiosity.

The father laughed as he saw his daughter thus employed, but bid her choose the finest stuff to make herself a wedding kirtle; whilst he himself turned again to the peddler, asking news of the realm; and young Edward leaned his elbows on

Evelyn Everett-Green

the table with his head in his hands, listening eagerly to every word that passed.

Paul almost wished he would not thus listen, for it was the same old story everywhere: discontent at the present state of things; longing for "the king"—by which was meant Edward the Fourth—to come back and reclaim the kingdom; gloomy prognostications of civil war; hopes that the proud Earl of Warwick would change sides once more—a thing many quite expected of him.

And invective against the feeble Henry and the warlike and revengeful Margaret of Anjou, scornfully called "the Frenchwoman," ran so high that Paul presently drew his kinsman away, and tried to interest him in other matters.

"Heed them not, my lord," he whispered. "We know there have ever been two factions in the kingdom, and in these parts they are all for the House of York. But the coming of this peddler may be good for you. Said you not that you wished to purchase a riding dress? His wares are good and not too costly for narrow purses. Since we mean to ride to London shortly, this were no bad time to furnish yourself with such things as you need for the journey."

Edward roused himself with an effort, and shook off the melancholy which had crept over his face as he listened to the talk round the table. The peddler's wares were being unpacked and handed round for inspection in a free and easy fashion enough; but the man made no objection, and only kept a pretty keen watch upon his property, glancing from time to time at the stranger youth with rather marked scrutiny, which, however, the latter did not observe.

There was a riding dress amongst the goods of the peddler somewhat similar to the one recently purchased by Paul, and

Edward decided upon the purchase of it, if he could come to terms with the man. He and Paul both desired to make some present to the bride, and picked out, the one an elegant high-peaked headdress, such as the ladies of the day loved to wear, though satirists made merry at the expense of their "exalted horns;" the other, some of the long gold pins to fasten both cap and hair which were equally acceptable as an adjunct to a lady's toilet.

Edward brought his purchases over to the corner where the peddler had ensconced himself, and addressed him in a low tone:

"See here, my good fellow. I am a wanderer from foreign parts; and my servant, who had charge of my moneybag, lost his life, I fear me, in trying to effect the landing on these shores, which I was lucky enough to manage in safety. Thus it comes about that I have but little gold about me. But your trade is one that barters all kinds of gear, and I have this pearl clasp to offer to you in part exchange for what I wish to take of you, so doubtless you will furnish me over and above with money to put in my gipsire: for the clasp is a valuable one, as any one who knows gems can see at a glance; nor would I part with it, but that necessity compels me."

The peddler looked at the clasp attentively, and then gave such a quick, keen look at the prince as would have aroused Paul's anxiety had he been near at hand. But he had not observed his comrade's last move, and was still patiently holding out stuffs in good natured if rather clumsy man fashion for the farmer's wife and daughter to take stock of and compare one with another.

"Hum—yes—a pretty trinket and a costly one, I doubt not, for those that have a market for such things," returned the peddler. "And how came you by it, young sir? It scarce

Evelyn Everett-Green

seems in accord with the simplicity of your dress and appointments."

Edward flushed slightly. He was not used to being taken to task, and that by a common peddler; but his common sense told him that he must expect such treatment now, and not be over ready to take offence, so he answered quietly enough:

"It has been in our family these many years. I know not how it came there first. I trow I am not the only youth who has jewels by him in these days little in keeping with the bravery of his other garments."

The peddler nodded his head with a smile.

"True, true, young sir; I meant no offence. Fortunes are lost and won but too quickly in these times, and will be again, I misdoubt me, ere England sees peace and prosperity once more. But at least the vultures fatten if honest folks starve; and what care princes how their subjects suffer, so as they and their nobles divide the spoil?"

"Nay, now, you wrong them," cried the lad with sudden heat. "He is unworthy the name of prince who could thus think or act."

Then pulling himself up quickly, as if afraid he had said too much, he returned to the matter of the bargain, and asked what the peddler would allow for the jewel.

The offer was not a very liberal one, but the man professed that jewels were difficult to get rid of, and Edward was no hand at making a bargain. However, when he had paid for his purchases he had a few gold pieces to put in his pouch, and he reflected that in London he should be able to dispose of the other jewels in his possession to better advantage. He had enough now to purchase a horse to take him to London, and for the present that was all he required.

He and Paul shared the same room at night, and talked in low tones far on into the small hours. Edward, who had suffered many hardships and privations since leaving the French court, was glad enough of a few days' rest in the hospitable farmhouse, and of the opportunity of hearing all the village gossip which the wedding festivity would give him. But after that event he desired to push on to London, to learn what he could of public feeling in the great metropolis.

"For, Paul," he said, gravely and almost sadly, "the city of London is like the heart of the nation. If that beat with enmity to our cause and love to our foes, I fear me all is lost before a blow has been struck. I know we have loyal friends in the west, and in some of those fair towns like Coventry and Lichfield; but if London be against us, that rich merchant city, the pride and wonder of the world, I have little heart or hope of success. Folks ever talk as if London were Yorkist to the core; but I yet have hopes that amongst her humbler citizens there may beat hearts warm in Henry of Lancaster's cause. At least I will go thither and see with my own eyes, and hear with my own ears. Disguised as we shall be, we shall hear the truth, and all men who are lukewarm will be inclining toward the cause that has the mighty King Maker, as they call him, in its ranks. We shall hear the best that is to be heard. If the best be bad, I shall know that our cause is hopeless indeed."

Paul pressed the hand he held, but said nothing. He feared only too well what they would hear in London. But yet, inasmuch as he was young and ardent, he hoped even whilst he feared; and talking and planning their future in glowing colours, both the lads fell asleep.

Evelyn Everett-Green

The following days were bright and busy ones at the farm. The peddler had vanished ere the travellers were downstairs next morning; but they had bought all they required overnight, and did not trouble about that. There was a great stirring throughout the house, and the needles of mistress and maid were flying swiftly whilst the short daylight lasted.

Edward and Paul spent the morning hours in the selection of a horse fit to carry the prince on his journey to London, and the farmer's son brought all the spare colts and lighter steeds into the straw yard for their guest to try and select for himself. There was no horse quite so handsome or well bred as Sultan, and Paul was eager for Edward to accept his steed in place of another. But the prince only laughed and shook his head, in the end selecting a fine chestnut colt only just broken to the wearing of the halter; and the kinsmen spent the best part of the next days in teaching the mettlesome though tractable creature how to answer to the rein and submit to saddle and rider. It was shod at Ives's forge, and christened by the name of Crusader, and soon learned to love the lads, who, whilst showing themselves masters of its wildest moods, were yet kindly and gentle in their handling.

The young prince was in great spirits during these days. He had been all his life somewhat too much under the close restraint of an affectionate but dictatorial mother, and had been master of none of his own actions. Such restraint was galling to a high-spirited youth; and although the sweetness of disposition inherited from his father had carried the prince through life without rebellion or repining, yet this foretaste of liberty was very delightful, and the romance of being thus unknown and obscure, free to go where he would unquestioned and unmarked, exercised a great fascination over him, and made him almost forget the shadow which sometimes seemed to hang over his path.

Paul was as light hearted as his companion in the main, though there were moments when his joy at having his adored prince under his care was dashed by the feeling of responsibility in such a charge, and by the fear of peril to the hope of the House of Lancaster. He wondered if it were his fancy that the farm was watched; that there were often stealthy steps heard without in the night—steps that set the dogs barking furiously, but which never could be accounted for next day; that if he rode or walked down the cart road to the village alone or with his comrade, their movements were followed by watchful eyes—eyes that seemed now and again to glare at him, as in the dusk that first evening, but which always melted away into the shadows of the forest if looked at closely or followed and tracked.

He was disposed to think it all the trick of an excited imagination, but he began to be not sorry that the day for departure was drawing near. If he had provoked the enmity of the robber chief, or if by a remoter chance the identity of his companion had been suspected, it would be better to be off without much more delay so soon as the wedding should be over.

Joan herself was nervous and fearful, and seldom set foot outside the door of her home. She sometimes said with a shiver that she was certain there were fierce men hiding about the house ready to carry her off if she did; and though her father and brother laughed at her fear, they humoured her, and were willing enough to let her keep safe at home: for Simon Dowsett was not a man to be trifled with, and he might very likely have heard before now that the woman he had vowed to make his wife was to be given in marriage to his rival.

The days, however, fled by without any event to arouse real disquiet, and on the morrow Joan would pass to the sturdy

Evelyn Everett-Green

keeping of the young smith, whose new house stood well flanked between his father's dwelling and the forge in the heart of the village where law-abiding persons dwelt in fair security.

The eve of the marriage day had come and gone. The household had retired to rest. Paul and Edward were in their raftered room, which was better lighted by the fire of logs than by the feeble rush light glimmering on the table. Fuel was so plentiful in that wooded country that all the hearths blazed in cold weather with the sputtering pine logs, which gave out an aromatic scent pleasant to the nostril.

As they closed the door behind them, Edward laid a hand upon his companion's arm and said:

"Good Paul, shall we two hold a vigil this night? I misdoubt me that some mischief is meditated toward Mistress Joan this night. I would that we might keep watch and ward."

"With all my heart," answered Paul readily, instinctively laying his hand upon his poniard. "But what makes you think that evil is intended?"

"I scarce know, but so it is. Noted you not how quiet and sluggish the dogs were at suppertime tonight? They would scarce come to receive a morsel of meat, and as often as not turned away in indifference, and curled themselves to sleep again. Indoors and out they are all alike. And did you not hear Jack Devenish say as he came in from his last round that he feared the great black watchdog in the yard would not live till morning, he seemed so sick and out of sorts? I wondered then that no one thought strange hands had been tampering with them; but all the farmer said was that he supposed they had gorged themselves upon the refuse meat of the sheep they had been killing—and I liked not to say ought to alarm them, for it may be as they say, and surely they ought best to know."

"Nevertheless we may well make ourselves watchdogs for tonight," said Paul. "If evil is meant against the girl, this is the last chance that bold Devil's Own, as they call him, will have of getting her into his power. They all call him a desperate fellow, and he will know that after the hard day's toil to have all in readiness for the morrow the household will sleep sound tonight. Why, even the maid had sleeping draught of spiced wine given her by her mother, that she might look her best in her bridal kirtle tomorrow. I think they all pledged themselves in the same bowl.

"I warrant there will be no watchers but ourselves tonight. What say you to look to our weapons and take the task upon ourselves?"

Edward's eyes gave ready response. What youths do not love the idea of facing the foe, and outwitting the cowardly cunning of those who have planned an attack upon a sleeping household? Paul thought he had been right now in fancying the house watched; but probably the hope of the watchers had rather been to find and carry off the girl than to take vengeance upon himself. He understood it all now, and was eager to defeat them a second time.

The nights were almost at their longest now, and the cold was very great; but the watchers piled fresh logs upon the fire, and talked quietly to each other as they sat in the dancing glow—for the rushlight had long since gone out. Midnight had passed. All was intensely still, and sleep seemed disposed to steal upon their senses in spite of their resolution to banish his presence. Paul was just about to suggest to his companion that he should lie down awhile on the bed and indulge in a nap, whilst he himself kept watch

Evelyn Everett-Green

alone, when the prince laid a hand upon his arm, and gripped him tight in a fashion which told that his quick ears had heard something.

The next moment Paul heard the same himself—stealthy sounds as of approaching footsteps, which paused beneath the window and then seemed to steal round the house. It was useless to look out of the window, for the night was dark as pitch, and they themselves might be seen; but they glanced at each other, and Paul whispered excitedly:

"It is to Mistress Joan's room they will find their way. I heard a sound as though a ladder was being brought out. They will climb to her window, force it open, and carry her away.

"Hark! that was the whinny of a horse. They are mounted, and think to baffle pursuit by their speed and knowledge, of the wood. There is no time to lose. Call up the farmer and his son. I know which is Mistress Joan's room. I will keep guard there till you come."

Paul knew every inch of the house by heart; but Edward was less familiar with its winding passages and crooked stairs. However, he knew the position of the rooms occupied by the farmer and his son, and groped his way thither; whilst Paul, with more certain step, sped lightly along another passage toward the room in which he knew Joan slept, not far from the serving wenches, but by no means near the men of the place.

All seemed profoundly quiet as he moved through the sleeping house; but he had scarce reached the door of the maiden's room before he heard the sound of a startled, muffled cry.

In a second he had burst open the door and had sprung in.

The sight which met his gaze showed how truly he had guessed. The window was open, and upon a ladder, with his body half in the room, was a sooty-faced man, holding in his hand a flaring torch to light the movements of his companion. This companion was already in the room; he was in the very act of lifting from the bed the form of the bride elect, who was so wrapped and smothered in the bed clothes that she was unable either to cry aloud or to resist. Paul could not see the face of the ruffian who was thus molesting her, and knew not whether it was Simon Dowsett or another in his employ; but he was disposed to think it was the captain himself, from the stalwart proportions of his frame and the gigantic strength he plainly possessed, of which he had heard so many stories told.

This man was so engrossed in his efforts of lifting and carrying away the struggling girl that he did not know it was any voice but that of his companion which had uttered the exclamation he had heard; and Paul, seeing that his presence was undetected, rushed straight across the room toward the window, grasped the ladder in both hands, and before the astonished ruffian upon it had recovered his surprise sufficiently to grapple with him, had flung the ladder and its occupant bodily to the ground, where the man lay groaning and swearing on the frost-bound stones beneath.

The torch had fallen within the room, and Paul snatched it up and stuck it in a crevice of the boards, for he did not wish his other adversary to escape in the darkness. The man had uttered a great oath as he became aware that his occupation had been interrupted, and dropping his burden upon the bed, he turned furiously upon his opponent, so quickly and so fiercely that Paul had barely time to draw his poniard and throw himself into an attitude of defence before the man was upon him.

Evelyn Everett-Green

"You again!" he hissed between his teeth, as his well-directed blows fell one after the other, taxing Paul's strength and agility not a little in evading or diverting them. "Have I not enough against you without this? Do you know that no man thwarts Devil's Own who lives not bitterly to rue the day? I have your name down in a certain book of mine, young man, and some day you will learn the meaning of that word. If I kill you not now, it is but that I may take a more terrible vengeance later. Let me pass, I say, or I may lose patience and cleave your skull as you stand."

But Paul had no intention of letting this dangerous foe escape him. He stood directly before the door, and barred the robber's way. It might have gone ill with the lad in spite of his courage and address, for he was but a stripling and the robber a man of unwonted strength, and full of fury now at being thus balked; but the sound of hurrying feet through the house toward the scene of conflict told both the combatants that an end to the struggle was approaching.

Paul shouted to them to take care the prey did not escape by way of one of the many crooked stairways, with which doubtless he was familiar enough; and he, seeing that all hope of escape through the house was now at an end, and knowing that he should inevitably be overpowered by numbers if he waited longer, suddenly sprang backwards and rushed to the window. Although it was high above the ground, and the stones below were both slippery and hard, he vaulted out like a deer, landing on the prostrate body of his companion, who received him with an execration and a groan; and as Paul rushed after him, intensely chagrined at this unexpected escape, he was only in time to see him dash off into the forest, or rather to hear his steps crashing through the thicket, until the sound of a horse's steady gallop showed that he was off and away.

The whole household was crowding into the room in various stages of dishabille. The terrified Joan and the disappointed Paul had each to tell their tale. But whilst the parents bent over their daughter, soothing her terrors and calming her fears, Jack drew toward Paul and his comrade, and said in low tones:

"Simon Dowsett is not a foe to be set at defiance. I would counsel you to take horse with the first gleam of day, and gain another parish or the protection of London, at least, before he has recovered from his discomfiture. I say this not without regret, as I would fain keep you over our feast today; but—"

The comrades exchanged glances, and spoke in one breath:

"We understand: you have spoken kindly and well," they said. "If you can have the horses in readiness, we will ride off with the first streak of dawn. It will be best so for all."

And though Joan Devenish and Will Ives were made man and wife that very morning, Paul and the prince were not there to grace the ceremony, but were far on their way to London.

CHAPTER 5

IN PERIL

"Edward, I am glad to see you back. Where have you been these many hours? I have been watching and waiting, hoping you would come before nightfall. I am very anxious. I much fear that we are suspected—spied upon."

"Nay, now, what makes you think that?" asked young Edward, as he let himself be drawn within the small attic bedchamber in the river-side inn, which he and his comrade had shared ever since they had arrived in London; now some three weeks back. Paul had closed the door before he began to speak, and now stood with his back against it, his face looking pale and anxious in the fading light of the winter's day.

"What makes me think it? Why, more things than one; but mainly the fact that the peddler we bought our clothes of is here."

Edward smiled and laid a hand on Paul's shoulder.

He was growing used to the anxieties of his elder comrade, who deeply felt his responsibility in having the heir of England under his care, and had begun to treat his words of warning with some lightness.

"And why should not the old man be here? The world is as free to him as it is to us. Rather I should have looked upon him as a friend. For did he not eat at the same board with us, and share the hospitality of the same roof?"

"Yes, yes," answered Paul quickly; "but so do all men of his calling. They are always welcome wherever they appear. But I will tell you why I misdoubt this man. He first came in whilst we of the house were sitting at dinner, and his eye roved round the room till it fell upon me, and I saw in it then a gleam of recognition which I did not like. He went out then, and anon returned with a great bearded fellow of sinister aspect. And I was certain that he pointed me out to him; for though I would not raise my eyes, or seem to notice, I knew that they whispered together, and that this other man's black eyes were fixed full on my face."

"That might well be," answered Edward lightly, "you are a right goodly youth, made to find favour in all eyes."

But Paul proceeded without heeding the interruption.

"Presently the peddler shuffled round the table, and took the vacant seat beside me—the seat that should have been yours, Edward. He pretended that he had only just recognized me, and began to talk in friendly fashion enough. He asked after you; but I said we had little companionship now—that you had your own concerns to attend to in the city, and that we might part company at any time. I would have disclaimed you altogether, save that those at the inn could have told him that I had a brother or comrade with me. He kept his eye warily on me the whole time. I know that he was on the watch for news of you."

"And wherefore not? Methinks you are over fearful, good Paul."

"Nay, Edward, think but a moment—What care would any feel for news of you did they not suspect something? Who cares whither I go or what I do? If you were but the obscure stranger you pass for, who would trouble to heed whither your steps were bent or how your time was passed? As you came in just now, did any man see you pass the threshold?"

"Nay, I know not. I was heeding little in the street. It was dark enough in the narrow alley, darker than it is up here; but—"

"Wait, Edward, answer me one question yet. Is it possible that the peddler can have any clue by which he may know you? Did you betray aught to him that evening when you bartered with him for your suit of clothes? How did you pay him? Was it in French gold?"

"Nay, I paid him no money at all. I gave him a pearl clasp which I had, and he furnished me with funds for the journey to London. I made a villainous bad bargain, it seems. The other jewels I have disposed of in London I have got far better price for.

"Now, Paul, why look you so troubled and wan? Have you yet another lecture in store for your luckless comrade?"

"O Edward, Edward," cried Paul in anxious tones, "is it really so? Have you been mad enough to sell jewels which may be known and traced? Did I not tell you from the very first that I had money enough for both? You should not have done it. And why, if done it must be, did you not tell me, and let me do the trafficking?"

Edward smiled as he laid his hand upon his comrade's shoulder.

"Good Paul, did you think that I would trade upon your love, to filch from you the remains of that poor fortune which is all you have left of the world's goods? I knew how readily your all would have been laid at my feet; but it was not for me to accept the sacrifice when I had means of raising money myself. And what danger can there be? My mother's jewels can scarce be known here. I fear your courage is but a sorry thing, you are so prone to idle fears and gloomy portents."

"Heaven grant I may be deceived; But the pearl clasp of which you speak—tell me what it was like."

"Why, a fine pearl set in a clasp of chased gold with an eagle in relief, the claws forming the catch of the clasp. My royal mother had a pair of them once; what befell the other I remember not. It was lost, I have heard her say, long years ago."

Paul clasped his hands closely together.

"Edward," he said, "it was just such a clasp as that which fastened the jewelled collar of the little Prince of Wales on the day when he, in play, fastened that collar about my neck, which collar fell a prey to certain robbers who carried off the humble knight's son in mistake for the prince.

"And listen further, Edward. Those same robbers who dogged your steps years ago are now in hiding in the fastnesses of that great Epping Forest through which we have lately journeyed. The peddler knows them and traffics with them; that have I heard from others. Most likely he has himself suspected something, and has gone with his clasp to consult with the chieftain, who is a sworn foe to the House of Lancaster. And having made out that the clasps are fellows, and having their suspicions fully aroused, they have followed

　　　　Evelyn Everett-Green

on our trail—we made no secret that London was our goal—and are seeking to get you into their power."

Edward's face was grave now. It seemed as if Paul's fears were not unfounded.

"Yet what good would come to them by that?" he questioned thoughtfully; and Paul had the answer only too ready.

"Marry, every good in the world! Dear my lord, forgive the plain speaking of one who loves you well; but we have not lived in this great city all these weeks for nought. You know how it is with the people of this land. They will never be ruled long by your saintly father. They know his strange malady, and they think him more fit for a monk's cell than a royal throne. Your mother—"

"Ay, they hate her," answered Edward mournfully. "They cannot speak her name without all manner of insulting epithets, which have made my blood boil in my veins."

"It is so, dear my lord; they have never loved her, and evil report will spread and gather head, You see that they would never accept her rule in your royal father's name. It would raise sedition and tumult at once. The house and faction of York know this. They know that their power would be secure were King Henry and his queen alone in the matter; but there is still one more—the Prince of Wales, against whom no man speaks evil, even the most rancorous enemies of the House of Lancaster. All who have seen him love him; all speak of his noble person, his graces of body and mind, his aptness to rule, his kingly qualities.

"You smile, but in truth it is so. The nation might rally beneath the banner of such a prince; and the proud nobles of the rival king know it well, and could they get the prince into their own power, they know that victory is from that moment theirs. Wherefore, Edward, if it be true that you are known, we must fly, and that instantly. These lawless men will not quit the trail till they have run the quarry down, and delivered you dead or alive into the hands of the foe. They know well the value of the prize, and they will not let it escape them."

Edward felt the truth of these words. Paul had been anxious and alarmed before, but never with the same cause. He had always been fearful that the young prince might be recognized by some wayfarer, who might have chanced to see him in past days or at the French court; but he had never before made sure that this recognition had actually taken place, and the likeness between the supposed brothers, though more a likeness now in figure and colouring and expression than actually in feature, was as great a safeguard as could have been devised.

Moreover, not a rumour of any kind had come over from France reporting the escape or absence of the Prince of Wales, and it was far fetched to imagine that anybody would suspect the identity of the yellow-haired youth. But the occurrences of this day, combined with Edward's admission about the clasp, had roused Paul's worst fears, and it did indeed seem as if there were some watch set upon their movements now.

He looked earnestly into the flushed face of the fair young prince, and then said thoughtfully:

"Edward, I have a plan whereby I think you can escape this threatened danger. Leave this house tonight—at once, if the coast be clear—and go as fast as your steed can take you to your royal father, and claim the protection of his state, and that of the earl your future father-in-law. Tell all your story, and it will make of you the idol even of this wayward city of London. All men will delight in the presence of the Prince of the Silver Swan; and methinks a happy end may be the result of the journey which seems like to end in peril and gloom.

"Good my lord, it is a joyous welcome you would receive. It would rejoice the whole heart of the nation to have you back."

Edward hesitated for a moment, but finally shook his head.

"Nay, Paul, I will not do that, though I grant the scheme has its attractions. If what you say be true and my presence in this city is suspected, be sure that every alley to the palace is watched and guarded by foes who would find a speedy way of preventing my entrance there—ay, or thine, were that tried.

"And over and above the danger, I am yearning to see the face of my sweet bride again, my gentle Anne, whom I have loved right well these many years, even whilst her father seemed our bitterest foe. My return will be looked for ere the glad Christmas season, and if I am not missed before, I shall be then, and I would not that my good mother were kept long in anxiety as to what has befallen me. I have been now four weeks absent. I laid careful plans whereby a brief absence might not be discovered, but it is time I returned now.

"Moreover, my quest is done. I have learned all and more than I came to do. My heart is heavy within me as I think on all I have heard. Ere I come as prince to this realm, I would fain see and have earnest speech with my mother. There are moments when methinks it would be the wiser and happier thing to talk no more of ruling here, but rather of securing to my father liberty and honour, and such titles and estates as he can claim through his duchy of Lancaster, and letting the crown remain on the head of him who could have claimed it with a better right than we, were it not for the kingly rule of my grandsire and his sire before him."

Paul made no reply save what was expressed in a deep sigh. His hope of the permanent restoration of the House of Lancaster had received some rude shocks during the past weeks; but he had never before heard Edward speak in this key, and he wondered if it were but the expression of a passing emotion, or the result of a deeply-seated conviction.

"I trow my mother will call me craven-hearted," said the lad with a slight smile, after a moment's silence, "and I myself may think differently anon. But tonight all seems wrapped in gloom, and I would I were far away from this city, which seems to breathe hatred to all of our name and race. Paul, we had better linger here no longer. Let us away the route we came, so shall we soonest reach the coast; and we will pass together to the French court, and you shall see the reception which will await us there from my mother and my sweet betrothed.

"Ah, I would the day had come! I long to see kindly faces once again. And they will love you ever for the love you have borne to me."

The lad's face flushed with excitement at the bare thought, and the prospect was welcome enough to Paul, who was sick at heart, and weary with the strain of continual watchfulness; but he lowered his voice to a mere whisper as he said:

"Hist, sweet prince! speak not so loud. There may be spies without the very door. We will indeed make shift to start the very first moment we may. I shall not draw another easy breath till we are far away from here. But think you it will be wise to go the way we came? May not those roads be

Evelyn Everett-Green

watched more closely there than elsewhere?"

"I think not so. I think they will guess that we shall make for one of the southern ports, by which France can be the more easily reached. If these wild robbers have left their former haunts to pursue us, we may well be safest nearest to their lair. And we know not the country to the south, whilst this great forest seems like a friend to us; and we have sturdy friends within its sheltering aisles if we are hard pressed. We can quicker reach the coast, too, that way than any other. And the good brothers you have spoken of at Leighs Priory will give us shelter tomorrow night, if we cannot make shift to push on to the coast in one day."

There seemed sound sense in the counsel thus offered by the prince, and Paul was ever ready to obey his wishes, if he saw no objection to them. They appeared to be menaced by peril on all sides, and he would have been thankful if the prince would have thrown himself into the keeping of his kingly sire; but as he had declined to do this, and was not of the stuff to be balked of his will, the next best thing was to slip off in silence and secrecy, and Paul thought it quite probable that the route least watched and guarded might well be the one which led back through the forest again.

But it would not do to appear as if suspicious; and leaving Edward locked up in the attic chamber—hoping that no one had observed his entrance into the inn—he went down into the common room, where preparations for supper were going on.

There were a larger number of persons collected in the inn than usual that night, and Paul fancied that many sharp glances were fastened upon him as he entered the room. But he kept command over his countenance well, and walked forward toward the fire with an air of easy assurance. The peddler was sitting in the warmest corner, and pushed away his next neighbour to make room for Paul, who took the vacant seat readily. The man very quickly led up to the subject of his companion and kinsman (laying an apparent and rather suspicious emphasis on that word), asking if he did not mean to come to supper, since he had seen him enter the inn at dusk.

Paul replied that his comrade was unwell, and that he would retire early to bed, and have something hot to take there. He was resolved that Edward should not be exposed to the gaze of these rough men, whose faces inspired him with the greatest uneasiness.

Edward should be supposed to be sick, and that might divert attention from his movements for the time being; and, long before the morning dawned, he hoped that they might both be far away from this ill-omened spot.

"Ill!" quoth the peddler; "no doubt a colic or a chill, taken in this villainous cold weather. I have a draught here that acts like a charm in all such cases. If you will permit me, I will mix it for you in a stoup of hot spiced wine, and I warrant he will sleep like a dormouse all night, and wake in the morning as well as ever."

Paul thanked the peddler, and the ingredients of the draught were called for. He watched its preparation keenly, and noted that several meaning glances were exchanged between the peddler and his associates—as he now believed half the men in the inn to be. He told the landlord to prepare two trenchers to be carried upstairs, as he would sup with his friend that night; and he presently carried up the hot and steaming tankard, together with the platters of the savoury viands for which London was famous.

Edward had meantime kindled the rushlight and set light to a small fire on the hearth, for the weather was bitterly cold. The peddler had advised Paul to partake of the hot draught also, and the landlord had not heeded his request to place a tankard of ale on the tray also: so that if either of the youths were to drink at all, it must be of the potion concocted by the peddler.

This fact greatly increased Paul's suspicions, which were quickly shared by Edward.

"We will not touch a drop of it," he said, "although it is tempting enough this cold night. It is either drugged or poisoned, and given us to keep us a certain prey for tonight. Perhaps in the end it will prove our best friend; for if they think us tied by the heel, they may be less vigilant in the watch they keep upon us."

It was not with much appetite that the comrades ate their supper, but they knew that they might need all their strength before the next hours had passed, and they ate heartily from that motive. Their trenchers had been so liberally piled, however, that there was plenty of broken meat and bread left when they had finished, and this was first allowed to grow cold, and then packed away into one of their wallets, as it might be some considerable time before they tasted food again, save such as they had with them.

Paul made several excursions from the room to ask for this thing or that, keeping up the fiction that his comrade was sick; and each time he did so he found some person or another guarding the door—at least watching hard by—though apparently bent upon some private errand. He came to the conclusion at last that their movements were most certainly spied upon, and that to attempt to escape through the house that night would be impossible. A few cautious words (which he caught as he entered the room where the peddler and his companions were sitting) confirmed his impression that Edward was certainly suspected, if not actually identified, and that he would not be allowed to pass out of sight until suspicion was either verified or laid at rest. He fancied, from the few words he heard, that these men were awaiting a companion who would be able absolutely to identify the prince, if it were really he, and that meantime they did not intend that either of the youths should escape their surveillance.

It was with a sinking heart that Paul returned to Edward with this news. But peril seemed only to act like a tonic upon the nerves of the younger lad; and springing to his feet with energy and resolution, he cried with flashing eyes:

"And so they think to make a prisoner of the eaglet of England's royal house! Let them try. Let them do their worst. They shall see that his wings are strong enough for a higher and more daring flight than they dream of; that he will not be fettered by a cage of their treacherous making! Paul, it is not for nothing that I have lain awake long nights dreaming dreams of peril and escape. I know how we will outwit our pursuers this very night. Say, can yon swim, as you can do all else that a brave Englishman should?"

"Like a fish," answered Paul, who had many a time terrified and astonished his mother by his feats in the salmon pool at home, and had never lost the skill and strength to battle with wind or wave.

"Good! I was sure of it; and I can do the same. Paul, come here to the window. See you no means of escape as you look down into that dark, sullen water below?"

Paul started and looked eagerly out. The inn, as has before been said, stood on the banks of the great river Thames.

Indeed, it was built so close to the waterside that the walls were washed by the lapping waves on the backside of the house, and the windows looked sheer down into the turbid, sullen stream. No watch could be kept on this side, nor did it seem to be needful; for the old inn was a lofty building of its kind, and the black water lay some sixty feet below the small window of the room in which Paul and his companion lodged. No man in his senses, it seemed, would hazard such a leap, and none but an expert swimmer would care or dare to trust himself to that swiftly-flowing flood, which might so easily sweep him to his doom. And on a freezing December night the idea of escape in such a fashion seemed altogether madness itself.

Even Paul, menaced by a danger that might be worse than death, drew in his head with something of a shudder; but Edward had dived into a little press that stood in the room, and brought out a coil of stout, strong rope. Paul gave a cry of surprise and pleasure.

"Some instinct warned me it might be wanted. See here, Paul. We can tie one end to this heavy bedstead, knotting it also around the bolt of the door, and we can glide down like two veritable shadows, and drop silently into the river: Then we must swim to one of those small wherries which lie at anchor beside the sleeping barges. I know exactly what course to steer for that; and once aboard, we cut her loose, and row for dear life down with the tide, till we can find some deserted spot where we can land, and thence we make our way back to the coast through the friendly forest, as we planned."

"On foot?"

"Ay, we must leave our good steeds behind; it would be madness to seek to take them. We are young and strong, and this frost makes walking easy. We shall speed so well that we may chance to reach the shelter of the Priory ere night falls on us again, and then the worst of our troubles will be over. Say, Paul, will you come with me? Will you follow me?"

"To the death, my prince," answered Paul with enthusiasm; yet even as he spoke a sort of shiver came over him, as though he had pronounced his own doom. But he shook it off, and fell to upon the simple preparations to be made.

These were very simple, and consisted of rolling up into a compact bundle their outer dress and a change of under tunic, which they fastened, together with their food wallet and arms, upon their heads, in the hope that they might keep them from the water. They slung their boots about their necks, and then, with as little clothing as possible upon them, commenced their stealthy descent down the rope, which had been firmly attached as suggested by the prince. Edward went first, whilst Paul remained in the room to guard against surprise, and to hold the end if it slipped or gave. But no such casualty befell; and the moment he heard the slight splash which told that the prince had reached the water, he swung himself lightly down the rope, and fell with a soft splash beside him.

But oh, how cold it was in that dark water! Hardy though the pair were, it seemed impossible to live in that fearful cold; but they struck out valiantly into midstream, and presently the exercise of swimming brought a little life into their benumbed limbs. But glad indeed was Paul to reach the side of the little wherry which they intended to purloin, and it was all that their united efforts could do to clamber in and cut the cord which bound it to the barge.

"We must row hard, Edward," said Paul, with chattering teeth; "it is our only chance of life. We shall freeze to death

Evelyn Everett-Green

if we cannot get some warmth into our blood. I feel like a block of ice."

They were too much benumbed to try and dress themselves yet, but as they rowed their hardest along the dark, still water, the life came ebbing back into their chilled limbs, and with the welcome warmth came that exultation of heart which always follows escape from deadly peril. With more and more vigour they bent to their oars, and at last Edward spoke in a natural voice again.

"Let us float down quietly with the stream a while, Paul, whilst we don our dry garments, if indeed they are dry. It will be better here than on shore, where we might chance to be seen and suspected. I am glowing hot now, freezing night though it be; but I confess I should be more comfortable rid of these soaking clothes."

So stripping off these, they found, to their great satisfaction, that the leather jerkins in which the other clothing had been wrapped had kept everything dry, and the feel of warm and sufficient clothing was grateful indeed after the icy bath they had encountered. Their boots were wet, but that mattered little to the hardy striplings; and when, dressed and armed, they bent to their oars again, it seemed as if all their spirit and confidence had come back.

"We have made so good a start that we shall surely prosper," cried Edward boldly. "Our good friend the peddler will look blank enough when morning comes and they find the birds are flown."

But Paul could not triumph quite so soon; he was still far from feeling assured of safety, and feared their escape might be quickly made known, in which case pursuit would be hot. The best hope lay in getting into the forest, which might give them shelter, and enable them to baffle pursuit; but responsibility lay sore upon him, and he could not be quite as gay as his comrade.

The moon shone out from behind the clouds, and presently they slipped beneath the arches of the old bridge, and past the grim fortress of the Tower. Very soon after that, they were gliding between green and lonely banks in a marshy land, and they presently effected a landing and struck northward, guiding themselves by the position of the moon.

It was a strange, desolate country they traversed, and glad enough was Paul that it was night when they had to cross this unprotected fiat land. By day they would be visible for miles to the trained eye of a highwayman, and if pursued would fall an easy prey. But by crossing this desolate waste at night, when not a living thing was to be seen, they might gain the dark aisles of the wood by the time the tardy dawn stole upon them, and once there Paul thought he could breathe freely again.

All through the long hours of the night the lads trudged onwards side by side. Paul was more anxious than weary, for he had been inured to active exercise all his life, and had spent many long days stalking deer or wandering in search of game across the bleak hillsides. But Edward, though a hardy youth by nature, and not altogether ignorant of hardship, had lived of late in the softer air of courts, and as the daylight struggled into the sky he was so weary he could scarce set one foot before another.

Yet even as Paul's anxious glance lighted on him he smiled bravely and pointed onwards, and there before them, in the rising sunlight, lay the great black forest, stretching backwards as far as eye could see; and Edward, throwing off his exhaustion by a manful effort, redoubled his speed, until the pair stood within the encircling belt of forest land, and paused by mutual consent at the door of a woodman's cabin.

Travellers were rare in that lone part, but the good folks of the hut were kindly and hospitable and unsuspicious. Paul produced some small pieces of silver and asked for food and shelter for a few hours, as he and his comrade had been benighted, and had been wandering about in the darkness many hours. The fare was very coarse and homely, but the famished lads were not disposed to find fault; and the cabin, if close, was at least warm, and, when a peat fire had been lighted, was a not altogether uncomfortable place for wanderers like themselves.

As soon as his hunger was satisfied, Edward lay down upon the floor and was soon sound asleep; but Paul had no disposition for slumber, and sat gazing into the glowing turves with earnest, anxious eyes. The heir of England was in his care, and already probably sought in many directions by cruel and implacable foes. Until Edward were in safety, he himself should know no peace. And as if suddenly inspired by some new thought, he started up and went in search of the good woman of the cabin, with whom he held a long and earnest conversation.

When he came back to the other room, it was with a smile of satisfaction on his face and a queer bundle in his arms, and the old woman was looking with great wonderment at a gold piece lying on her palm, and marvelling at the strange caprice of the young and rich.

CHAPTER 6

IN THE HANDS OF THE ROBBERS

"But wherefore should I disguise myself rather than you?" cried Edward, resisting Paul's efforts to clothe him in a long smock frock, such as the woodmen of those days wore when going about their avocations. "Our peril is the same, and it is I who have led you into danger. I will not have it so. We will share in all things alike. If we are pursued and cannot escape, we will sell our lives dear, and die together. But let it never be said that I left my friend and companion to face a danger from which I fled myself."

The boy's eyes flashed as he spoke—he looked the very image of a prince; and Paul's heart swelled with loving pride, although he still persisted in his design.

"Listen, Edward," he said, speaking very gravely and resolutely. "It is needful for our joint safety that we be not seen together, now that we are entering a region of country where we may easily be recognized, and where watch may be kept for us. Yes, these woods may be watched, although, as you have said, it is probable they will watch even more closely the other routes to the coast. But we have come slowly, toiling along on foot, and there has been ample time for a mounted messenger to ride back and give the warning

Evelyn Everett-Green

to such of the robbers as are yet here. They know that the twain of us are travelling together. Wherefore, for the few miles that separate us now from the kindly shelter of the Priory, it will be better that we journey alone. This smock and battered hat will protect you from recognition, the more so when I have blackened your face with charcoal, as I have means to do, and have hidden away all your bright curls so that none shall see them. Walk with bent shoulders and heavy gait, as the aged country folks do, and I warrant none will guess who you are or molest you. Tonight, when we meet to laugh at our adventures over the prior's roaring fire, we shall forget the perils and the weariness of our long tramp."

"But, Paul, I love not this clumsy disguise. It befits not a prince thus to clothe himself. Wear it yourself, good comrade, for your peril is as great as mine."

"Nay, Edward, speak not thus idly," said Paul, with unwonted gravity. "Princes must think not of themselves alone, but of the nation's weal. Edward, listen. If harm befalls you, then farewell to all the fond hopes of half of the people who obey the sway of England's sceptre. You are not your own master; you are the servant of your loyal and true-hearted subjects, who have suffered already so much in the cause. To throw your life away, nay, even to run into needless peril, were a sin to them and to the country. I say nothing of your mother's despair, of the anguish of your bride, if harm befell you: that you must know better than I can do. But I am a subject. I know what your subjects feel; and were you to neglect any safeguard, however trivial, in these remaining hours of threatened danger, you would be doing England a wrong which might be utterly irreparable."

Edward was struck by this argument, and hesitated.

"I only wish to do what is right; but I cannot bear to play the coward's part, and save myself when you are still in peril."

"Tush!" answered Paul lightly, "I am tougher than you, Edward; you are so footsore and weary you can scarce put one leg before the other. If foes were to spring upon us, you would fall an easy prey at once. I am strong and full of life. I could lead them a fine chase yet. But we may never sight an adversary. These woods are still and silent, and we have heard no sounds of dread import all these long, weary miles. It may well be that we shall reach the Priory in safety yet; but it were better now to part company and take different routes thither. And you must don this warm though clumsy dress; it will keep you the safer, and shield you from the piercing cold, which you feel more than I do."

In truth, the youthful prince was nigh worn out from fatigue, notwithstanding the fact that Paul had contrived to give him almost the whole of their scanty provision, and had helped him tenderly over the roughest of the way. It was true, indeed, that had they been attacked Edward would have fallen an easy prey; but alone in this disguise, hobbling along with the heavy gait of an aged rustic, he would attract no suspicion from any robber band. And Paul was eager to see him thus equipped; for they had reached the part of the wood which was familiar to both, and the prince could easily find the shortest and most direct way to the Priory, whilst he himself would make a short circuit and arrive from another point with as little delay as possible.

A strong will and a sound argument generally win the day. Edward submitted at last to be arrayed in the woodman's homely garments, and was grateful for the warmth they afforded; for he was feeling the bitter cold of the northern latitude, and was desperately tired from his long day and night of walking. There was no pretence about the limping,

Evelyn Everett-Green

shuffling gait adopted; for his feet were blistered and his limbs stiff and aching.

Paul watched him hobbling away, his face looking swarthy and old beneath the shade of the hat, his shoulders bent, and his blackened hands grasping a tough ash stick to help himself along; and a smile of triumph stole over his own countenance as he heaved a long sigh of relief—for he felt quite certain that in the gathering dusk no one would suspect the true character of the weary pedestrian, and that he would reach the shelter of the Priory in safety.

It seemed as if a millstone were rolled from Paul's neck as he turned from contemplating that retiring figure. The strain upon his faculties during the past twenty-four hours had been intense, and when it was removed he felt an immense sensation of relief. But with that relief came a greater access of fatigue than he had been conscious of before. He had been spurred along the road by the sense of responsibility—by the feeling that the safety and perhaps the life of the young Prince of Wales depended in a great measure upon his sagacity, endurance, and foresight. To get the prince to Leigh's Priory, beneath the care of the good monks who were stanch to the cause of the saintly Henry, was the one aim and object of his thoughts. He had known all along that the last miles of the journey would be those most fraught with peril, and to lessen this peril had been the main purpose on his mind. Having seen the prince start off on the direct path, so disguised that it was impossible to anticipate detection, he felt as though his life's work for the moment were ended, and heaving a great sigh of relief, he sank down upon a heap of dead leaves, and gave himself up to a brief spell of repose, which his weary frame did indeed seem to require.

The cold, together with the exhaustion of hunger and fatigue, sealed his senses for a brief space, and he remembered nothing more. He fancied his eyes had been closed but for a few seconds, when some noise close at hand caused him to raise his head with a start. But the dusk had deepened in the great wood, and he saw that he must have been asleep for quite half an hour.

He started and listened intently. Yes, there was no mistaking the sounds. A party of mounted horsemen were approaching him along the narrow track which wandered through the wood. Paul would have started to his feet and fled to the thicket, but his benumbed limbs refused their office. It was freezing hard upon the ground, and he had lain there till his blood had almost ceased to circulate, and he was powerless to move.

Yet even then his thoughts were first for Edward, and only second for himself. He rapidly reviewed the situation.

"They are on the path that he has taken. He has the start, but they are mounted. Are they in pursuit of anyone? They have dogs with them: that looks as if they were hunting something. It were better that they should not come up with Edward. In another half hour he will be safe at the Priory, if he make good speed, as methinks he will; for with the hope of speedy ease and rest, even the weariest traveller plucks up heart and spirit. If they are following him, to find even me will delay them. If not, they will pass me by unheeded. I am not likely even to attract their notice. I cannot escape if I would. I am sore, weary, and chilled beyond power of flight, and the dogs would hunt me down directly. My best chance is to rest quiet and tranquil, as if I knew not fear. Perchance they then will let me go unscathed."

Possibly had Paul's faculties been less benumbed by fatigue and the bitter cold, he would scarce have argued the case so calmly; but he was calm with the calmness of physical

Evelyn Everett-Green

exhaustion, and in truth his chance of escape would have been small indeed. He could have made no real effort at flight, and the very fact of his trying to hide himself would have brought upon him instant pursuit and capture.

So he lay still, crouching in his nest of leaves, until one of the dogs suddenly gave a deep bay, and came rushing upon him, as if indeed he had been the quarry pursued.

"Halt there!" cried a deep voice in the gloom; "the dogs have found. They never give tongue for a different trail than the right one.

"Dicon, dismount and see what it is; there is something moving there be neath that bush."

Seeing himself discovered, Paul rose to his feet, and made a step forward, though uncertainly, as if his limbs still almost refused to obey him.

"I am a poor benighted traveller," he said; "I pray you, can you direct me where I can get food and shelter for the night? I have been wandering many hours in this forest, and am weary well-nigh to death."

"Turn the lantern upon him, fellows," said the same voice that had spoken before; and immediately a bright gleam of light was cast upon Paul's pale, tired face and golden curling hair.

"Is this the fellow we are seeking?" asked the leader of his followers; "the description seems to fit."

"If it isn't one it is the other," answered the man addressed. "I have seen both; but, marry, I can scarce tell one from the other when they are apart. What has he done with his companion? They have, been together this many a day, by day and by night."

"You were not alone when you started on this journey last night," said the robber, addressing Paul sternly. "Where is your companion? You had better speak frankly. It will be the worse for you if you do not."

Paul's heart beat fast; the blood began to circulate in his veins. He tried hard to keep his faculties clear, and to speak nothing which could injure the prince.

"We parted company. I know not where he is," he answered slowly. "I told him to go his own way; I would not be a source of peril to him. I bid him adieu and sent him away."

It suddenly occurred to Paul that if, even for an hour, he could personate the prince, and so draw off pursuit from him, his point might be gained. He had not forgotten the episode of the first adventure they had shared as children; and as we all know, history repeats itself in more ways than one.

The man who appeared the leader of the band, and whose face was not unkindly, doffed his hat respectfully at these words, and said, "It is true, then, that I am addressing the Prince of Wales?"

Paul said nothing, but bent his head as if in assent, and the man continued speaking, still respectfully.

"It is my duty then, sire, to take your sacred person under my protection. You are in peril from many sources in these lone woods, and I have been sent out on purpose to bring you into a place of safety. My followers will provide you with a good horse, and you will soon be in safe shelter, where you can obtain the food and rest your condition requires, and you will

Evelyn Everett-Green

receive nothing but courteous treatment at our hands."

To resist were fruitless indeed. Politely as the invitation was tendered, there was an undertone of authority in the man's voice which convinced Paul that any attempt at resistance would be met by an appeal to force. And he had no disposition to resist. The longer the fiction was kept up, the longer there would be for the prince to seek safe asylum at the Priory. When once those sanctuary doors had closed behind Edward, Paul thought it mattered little what became of himself.

"I will go with you," he answered with simple dignity; "I presume that I have indeed no choice."

A draught from a flask tendered him by one of the men did much to revive Paul, and the relief at finding himself well mounted, instead of plodding wearily along on foot, was very great. He was glad enough to be mounted behind one of the stout troopers, for he was excessively drowsy, despite the peril of his situation. He had been unable to sleep, as Edward had done, in the woodman's hut, and it was now more than thirty-six hours since sleep had visited him, and those hours had been crowded with excitement, peril, and fatigue. The potent liquor he had just drunk helped to steal his senses away, and as the party jogged through the dim aisles of the wood, Paul fell fast asleep, with his head resting on the shoulder of the stalwart trooper, and he only awoke with a start, half of fear and half of triumph—for he knew the prince was safe enough by this time—when the glare from the mouth of a great cavern, and the loud, rough voices of a number of men who came crowding out, smote upon his senses, and effectually aroused him to a sense of what was passing.

"Have you got them?" cried a loud voice, not entirely unfamiliar to Paul, although he could not for the moment remember where he had heard it before.

"We have got one-got the most important one," answered the man who had been leader of the little band. "The other has got off; but that matters less."

"By the holy mass, it was the other that I wanted the more," cried the rougher voice, as the man came out swearing roundly; "I had an account of my own to square with him, and square it I will one of these days. But bring in the prize—bring him in. Let us have a look at him. He is worth the capture, anyhow, as the Chief will say when he returns. He is not back yet. We have all been out scouring the forest; but you always have the luck, Sledge Hammer George. I said if any one brought them in it would be you."

Paul had by this time recognized the speaker, who was standing in the entrance of the cave with the light full upon his face. It was none other than his old adversary, Simon Dowsett, whom he had twice defeated in his endeavour to carry off the lady of his choice; and who was, as he well knew, his bitterest foe. His heart beat fast and his breath came fitfully as he realized this, and he looked quickly round toward the black forest, as if wondering if he could plunge in there and escape. But a strong hand was laid upon his arm, and he was pushed into the cave, where the ruddy glow of the fire fell full upon him.

Simon Dowsett, who in the absence of the Chief, as he was called, acted as the captain of the band, strode forward and fixed his eyes upon the lad, his face changing as he did so until its expression was one of diabolical malice.

"What?" he cried aloud; "at the old game again? You thought to trick us once more, and again to get off with a sound skin?—Lads, this isn't the prince at all; this is the other of them, who has fooled you as he fooled the Chief himself long years ago. What were you thinking of to take his word for it? And you have let the real one slip through your fingers.

"Ha, ha, Sledge Hammer George! you are not quite so clever as you thought. Why did you not wring the truth out of him, when the other quarry could not have been far off? You have been pretty gulls to have been taken in like this!"

The other man, who had now come up, looked full into Paul's face, and asked, not savagely though sternly enough:

"Which are you, lad? speak the truth. Are you the Prince of Wales, or not?"

It was useless now to attempt to keep up the deception. Paul carried the mark of Simon Dowsett's bullet in his shoulder, and he was too well known by him to play a part longer. Looking full at the man who addressed him, he answered boldly:

"I am Paul Stukely, not the prince at all. He is beyond the reach of your malice. He is in safe shelter now."

"Where is he?" asked the man quietly.

"I shall not tell you," answered Paul, who knew that these robbers were so daring that they might even make a raid on the Priory, or watch it night and day, and to prevent the escape of the prince from thence, if their suspicions were once attracted, to the spot.

Sledge Hammer George laid a hand upon the young man's arm.

"Now don't be a fool, lad; these fellows here will stand no

more from you. A valuable prize has escaped them, and they will wring the truth out of you by means you will not like, but will not be able to resist. You have a bitter enemy in Devil's Own, as he is called, and he will not spare you if you provoke. I will stand your friend, if you will but speak out and tell us where the prince is to be found; for he cannot be very many miles away from this place, as we are well assured. If you are obstinate, I can do nothing for you, and you will have to take your chance.

"Come, now, speak up. Every moment is of value. You will be made to do so before long, whether you wish or not."

Paul's lips closed tightly one over the other, and his hands clasped themselves fast together. He thought of the vow he had registered long years ago in his heart, to live or to die in the service of his prince; and though what he might be called upon to suffer might be far worse than death itself, his will stood firm, and he gave no sign of yielding. The man, who would have stood his friend if he would have spoken, looked keenly at him, and then turned away with a slight shrug of the shoulders, and Simon's triumphant and malicious face was looking into his.

"Now, lad, once more: will you speak, or will you not? It is the last time I shall ask you."

"I will tell you nothing," answered Paul, raising his head and looking at his old enemy with a contempt and lofty scorn which seemed to sting the man to greater fury.

"You will not! very good. You will be glad enough to speak before I have done with you. I have many old scores to settle with you yet, and so has the Chief when he comes back; but the first thing is to wring from you where the prince is hiding himself.

Evelyn Everett-Green

"Strip off his fine riding dress and under tunic, lads (it is a pity to spoil good clothes that may be useful to our own brave fellows), and string him up to that beam.

"Get out your hide whips, Peter and Joe, and lay it on well till I tell you to stop."

With a brutal laugh, as if it were all some excellent joke, the men threw themselves upon Paul, and proceeded to carry out the instructions of their leader, who seated himself with a smile of triumph where he could enjoy the spectacle of the suffering he intended to inflict. Paul's upper garments were quickly removed, and his hands and feet tightly bound with leather thongs. An upright and a crossway beam, supporting the roof of the cave, formed an excellent substitute for the whipping post not uncommon in those days upon a village green; and Paul, with a mute prayer for help and courage, nerved himself to meet the ordeal he was about to undergo, praying, above all things, that he might not in his agony betray the prince to these relentless enemies.

The thick cow-hide whips whistled through the air and descended on his bare, quivering shoulders, and he nearly bit his lips through to restrain the cry that the infliction almost drew from him. But he was resolved that his foe should not have the satisfaction of extorting from him any outward sign of suffering save the convulsive writhings which no effort of his own could restrain. How many times the cruel whips whistled through the air and descended on his back, he never knew—it seemed like an eternity to him; but at last he heard a voice say:

"Hold, men!"

"Dowsett, you will kill him before the Chief sees him, and that he will not thank you for. He is a fine fellow, and I won't stand by and see him killed outright. Take him down and lock him up safely till the Chief returns. He will say what is to be done with him next. It is not for us to take law into our own hands beyond a certain point. You will get nothing out of him, that is plain; he is past speech now."

"The Chief will make him find his tongue," said Dowsett with a cruel sneer; "this is only a foretaste of what he will get when the Fire Eater returns.

"Take him down then, men. 'Twere a pity to kill him too soon. Keep him safe, and we will see what the Chief says to him tomorrow."

Paul heard this as in a dream, although a merciful semi-consciousness had deadened him to the worst of the pain. He felt himself unbound and carried roughly along down some dark passage, as he fancied. There was a grating noise, as if a door had turned on its hinges, and then he was flung down on what seemed like a heap of straw, and left alone in pitchy darkness.

For a time he lay just as he had been thrown, in the same trance of semi-consciousness; but after what had appeared to him a very long time, he beheld as if a long way off a glimmering light, which approached nearer and nearer, though he was too dizzy and faint to heed its movements much. But it certainly approached quite close to him—he saw as much through his half-closed eyelids—and then a voice addressed him, a soft, sweet voice, strangely unlike those he had just been hearing.

"Are you indeed Paul Stukely?" asked the voice.

The sound of his name aroused him, and he made a great effort to see through the mists that seemed to hang over his eyes. A sweet and very lovely face was hanging over him. He thought he must be dreaming, and he asked faintly, hardly knowing what he said:

"Is it an angel?"

"Oh no, I am no angel, but only the daughter of the Chief; and I want to help you, because I have heard of you before, and I cannot bear that they should kill you by inches, as I know they will do if you stay here. See, they are all fast asleep now, and there is no chance of my father's return tonight. I have brought you your clothes, and Madge has given me some rag steeped in a concoction of herbs of her own making, which will wonderfully ease your wounds if you will let me lay it on them. Old Madge is a wonderful leech, and she cannot bear their cruel doings any more than I can, and she said you were a brave lad, and she made you some soup, which I will fetch for you to hearten you up for your journey. For you must get away from here before morning, or nothing can save you from a terrible fate.

"See now, do not your poor shoulders feel better for this dressing? If you can put your clothes on whilst I am gone, I will bring you something that will go far to help you over your ride tonight."

It was a great effort to Paul to collect his wandering faculties, and get his lacerated and trembling limbs to obey his will; but he was nerved to his utmost efforts by the dread of what might befall him if he could not avail himself of this strange chance of escape. By the time the fair-faced girl had returned with a steaming basin in her hands, he had contrived to struggle into his garments, and though quivering in every fibre of his being, was more himself again, and able to understand better the rapid stream of words poured out by the eager maiden.

"Drink this," she said, giving him the basin. "It is very good. It has all kinds of ingredients in it that will ease your pain and give you strength and courage; but that you have without. Oh, I think you are the bravest lad I ever knew. But listen, for I am going to tell you a strange story. I told you that I was the, daughter of the robber chief, did I not? Well, so I am; and my father loves me the more, I think, that he never loved any other being save my mother, and she died in this very cave when I was born. He has always loved me and given me my own way; but these last weeks a change seems to have come over him, and he talks of giving me in wedlock to that terrible man T hate worse than them all—the one they call Devil's Own. He has never spoken a soft word to me all these years; but the past three weeks he has tried to woo me in a fashion that curdles the very blood in my veins. I would not wed him were I heart whole as a babe; and I am not that, for my hand and heart are pledged to another, whose wife I will surely be."

The girl's eyes flashed, and it was plain that the spirit of the sire had descended to her. Paul was slowly swallowing the contents of the basin, and feeling wonderfully invigorated thereby; indeed, he was sufficiently restored to feel a qualm of surprise at being thus intrusted with the history of this young girl, and she seemed to divine the reason of his inquiring look.

"I will tell you why I speak thus freely; and I must be brief, for the moments fly fast, and it is time we were on our way. The man I love is one Jack Devenish, of a place they call Figeon's Farm; and this very night, ere my father returns, I am to meet him; and he will carry me to his home and his mother, and there shall I lie hid in safety until such time as the priest may wed us. And, Paul, it is a happy chance that brought you hither this night instead of another; for we will fly together, and you will be safe at Figeon's as I. For they

Evelyn Everett-Green

will not suspect whither we have fled, nor would they dare to attack a peaceful homestead near the village if they did. They have made this country almost too hot to hold them as it is, and are ever talking of a flight to the north. Methinks they will soon be gone, and then I can draw my breath in peace."

Paul listened in amaze. It was an effort to think of moving again tonight, so weary and worn and suffering was he; but anything was better than remaining behind in the power of these terrible men, and he rose slowly to his feet, though wincing with every movement.

"I know it pains you," cried the girl compassionately; "but oh, what is that pain to what you would have to endure if you were to stay? And you will not have to walk. My palfrey is ready tied up in the wood, a bare stone's throw from here. You shall ride her, and I will run beside you, and guide you to the trysting place, where my Jack will be awaiting me, and his great roan will carry the pair of us. Now silence, and follow me. There is a narrow exit from this inner recess in the cave known only to me and to Madge. Not one of the robbers, not even my father himself, knows of it. They think they have you in a safe trap, and will not even keep watch tonight after their weary search.

"Tread softly when you reach the open, lest our footsteps be heard. But it is far from the mouth of the cave, and I have never raised an alarm yet, often as I have slipped out unawares. Give me your hand—so; now stoop your head, and squeeze through this narrow aperture. There, here are we beneath the clear stars of heaven, and here is my pretty Mayflower waiting patiently for her mistress.

"Yes, pretty one; you must bear a heavier burden tonight, but you will do it gladly for your mistress's sake.

"Mount, good sir; we shall soon be out of reach of all danger."

It must be a dream thought Paul, as, mounted on a light palfrey, he went speeding through the dun wood by intricate paths, a fairy-like figure springing through the gloom beside him, and guiding the horse, as he was utterly unable to do.

It seemed as if his strength had deserted him. His hands had lost their power, and it was all he could do to maintain his seat on the animal that bounded lightly along with her unaccustomed burden. At last they reached an open glade; a dark, motionless figure was standing in the moonlight.

"It is he—it is my Jack!" cried the fairy, springing forward with a faint cry of welcome.

"O Jack, I have brought your old friend Paul Stukely back to you. You must take care of him as well as of me, for he has been in deadly peril tonight."

Evelyn Everett-Green

CHAPTER 7

THE PROTECTION OF THE PROTECTED

"Nay, wife, why sit up for him? Since he has taken to these roving habits at night there is no depending upon him. I must put an end to them if they are to disturb you so. The boy is safe enough. Why are you anxious about him tonight?"

It was Farmer Devenish who spoke these words to his wife, half an hour after the rest of the household had retired to rest, and he found her still sitting beside the fire, which she had piled up high on the hearth, as if she meant to remain downstairs for some time; which indeed she distinctly told him was her intention, as she did not wish to go to bed until Jack had come in.

"He asked me to sit up for him tonight," she answered, "and he never did so before. I was glad of it; for I have been uneasy for the boy, wondering what could take him out so often at night."

"Oh, he's going courting, you may depend upon it," laughed the farmer in his hearty way; "and courting some young lass not of our village, but one who lives a pretty step from here, I'll be bound. I've held my peace, and let the boy go his own way. He'll speak out when the time comes, depend upon it."

"I believe he will speak out this very night," answered the mother. "He told me he had a surprise in store for me, and begged that I would sit up till his return, and stand his friend with you, if you should be displeased at his choice. One might have thought he was bringing his bride home with him, to hear him talk; but he would never get wedded without speaking first. He is a good lad and a dutiful, and his parents have the right to be told."

The farmer's curiosity was piqued by what he heard, and he resolved to share his wife's vigil. Jack, their only son, was very dear to them, and they were proud of him in their own hearts, and thought such a son had never lived before. Both were anxiously looking forward to the day when he should bring home a wife to brighten up the old home, since it had lost the sweet presence of the daughter Joan; and they neither of them believed that Jack's choice would fall upon anyone unworthy of him.

The farmer dozed in his chair by the glowing hearth. The woman got a large book from some secret receptacle upstairs, and read with deep attention, though with cautious glance around her from time to time, as if half afraid of what she was doing. It was long before the silence outside was broken by any sound of approaching footfalls; and when the ring of a horse hoof upon the frosty ground became distinctly audible through the silence of the night, the farmer would not unbar the door until his wife had glided away with the volume she had been reading.

A minute later and the parents both stood in the doorway, peering out into the cloudy night, that was not altogether dark.

"By holy St. Anthony, there are two horses and three riders," said the farmer, shading his eyes from the glare of the lantern as he peered out into the darkness beyond.

"Jack, is that you, my son? And who are these that you have brought with you?"

"Friends—friends claiming the shelter and protection of your roof, father," answered Jack's hearty voice as he rode up to the door; and then it was seen that he was greatly encumbered by some burden he supported before him on his horse. But from the other lighter palfrey there leaped down a small and graceful creature of fairy-like proportions, and Mistress Devenish found herself suddenly confronted by the sweetest, fairest face she had ever seen in her life, whilst a pair of soft arms stole caressingly about her neck.

"You are Jack's mother," said a sweet, soft voice in accents of confident yet timid appeal that went at once to her heart. "He has told me so much of you—he has said that you would be a mother to me. And I have so longed for a mother all my life. I never had one. Mine own mother died almost ere I saw the light. He said you would love me; and I have loved you long. Yet it is not of myself I must talk now, but of yon poor lad whom you know well. We have brought Paul Stukely back to you. Oh, he has been sorely handled by those cruel robbers—the band of Black Notley! He has been like a dead man these last miles of the road. But Jack says he is not dead, and that your kindly skill will make him live again."

And before Mistress Devenish was well aware whether she were not in a dream herself, her husband had lifted into the house the apparently inanimate form of Paul Stukely, and had laid him down upon the oak settle near to the hospitable hearth.

Jack had gone to the stable with the horses; but one of the serving men having been aroused and having come to his assistance, he was able quickly to join the party beside the fire, and coming forward with a glad and confident step, he took the hand of the fairy-like girl in his own, and placed it within that of his mother.

"Father, mother," he said, "I have brought you home my bride that is to be. Listen, and I will tell you a strange story, and I know you will not then withhold your love from one who has known little of it, and who has led a strange, hard life amid all that is bad and cruel, and is yet all that you can wish to find in woman—all that is true and pure and lovely."

And then Jack, with the sort of rude eloquence sometimes found in his class, told of his wooing of the robber's daughter; told of her hatred and loathing of the scenes she was forced to witness, of the life she was forced to lead; told of her fierce father's fierce love gradually waning and turning to anger as he discovered that she was not pliable material in his hands, to be bent to his stern will; told how he had of late wished to wed her to the terrible Simon Dowsett, and how she had felt at last that flight alone with her own lover could save her from that fate.

Then he told of Paul's capture upon the very night for which the flight had been planned; told how gallantly he had defied the cruelty of the robber band, and how his Eva had effected his liberation and had brought him with her to the trysting place. They had planned before the details of the flight, and it would be death to her to be sent back; but after her liberation of the captive, the thought of facing that lawless band again was not to be thought of.

And the farmer, who had listened to the tale with kindling eyes and many a smothered ejaculation of anger and pity, suddenly put his strong arms about the slight figure of the girl, and gave her a hearty kiss on both cheeks.

Evelyn Everett-Green

"Thou art a good wench and a brave one," he said, "and I am proud that my roof is the one to shelter thee from those lawless men, who are the curse of our poor country.

"Jack, I told the mother that you must be going courting, and that I should be right glad when you brought a bride to the old home. And a bride this brave girl shall be as soon as Holy Church can make you man and wife; and we will love her none the less for what her father was. I always heard that the Fire Eater, as they call him, had carried off and married a fair maiden, too good by a thousand times for the like of him; and if this is that poor lady's daughter, I can well believe the tale. But she is her mother's child, not her fierce father's, and we will love her as our own.

"Take her to your heart, good mother. A brave lass deserves a warm welcome to her husband's home."

The gentle but high-spirited Eva had gone through the dangers of the night with courage and resolution, but tears sprang to her eyes at hearing these kindly words; and whilst Jack wrung his father's hand and thanked him warmly for his goodwill. The girl buried her face upon the shoulder of Mistress Devenish, and was once more wrapped in a maternal embrace.

And then, having got the question of Eva's adoption as Jack's betrothed bride so quickly and happily settled, they all turned their attention to poor Paul, who for a few minutes had been almost forgotten.

There was a warm little chamber scarce larger than a closet opening from the room where the farmer and his wife slept, and as there was a bed therein always in readiness against the arrival of some unlooked-for guest, Paul was quickly transported thither, and tenderly laid between the clean but coarse coverings. He only moaned a little, and never opened his eyes or recognized where he was or by whom he was tended; whilst the sight of his lacerated back and shoulders drew from the woman many an exclamation of pity, and from the farmer those of anger and reprobation.

It was some time before they understood what had happened, or realized that the young kinsman (as they had called him) of Paul's was really the Prince of Wales, the son of the now reigning Henry, and that the two lads had been actually living and travelling together with this secret between them. But Eva had heard much about both, and told how the presence of the prince in the country had become known to her father and his band first through the suspicions of the peddler, who had seen the one pearl clasp still owned and kept by the robber chief, and had at once recognized its fellow; and secondly, from the identification of Paul's companion with the Prince of Wales by one of the band who had been over to France not long ago, and had seen the prince there.

The old likeness between the two youths was remembered well by the band, who had been fooled by it before; and they had been for weeks upon the track of the fugitives, who had, however, left Figeon's before their enemies had convinced themselves of their identity; and in London they were less easily found. Eva did not know the whole story—it was Paul who supplied the missing links later; but she told how a great part of the band had gone forth to seek them in the city— how word had presently been brought by a mounted messenger that the fugitives had escaped, just when they were certain they had them fast—that all roads were being watched for them, but that those who still remained in the forest were to keep a close lookout, lest by some chance they should return by the way they had come.

Evelyn Everett-Green

The band had been scouring the woods all that day in different detachments, and they had brought in Paul just before dark. The prince had escaped their vigilance, and Paul had maintained silence under their cruel questioning. Eva knew no more of him than the farmer, but all were full of hope that he had escaped. Well indeed for both—if Paul knew his hiding place—that he was out of the power of the robbers. They would scarce in any case have let him escape with his life, after the ill will many of them bore him; but had he continued to set them at defiance by his silence, there is no knowing to what lengths their baffled rage might not have gone. Eva had heard of things in bygone days which she could not recall without a shudder, and the farmer and Jack, with clenched hands and stern faces, vowed that they would leave no stone unturned until the country was rid of these lawless and terrible marauders.

"We have stood enough; this is the last!" cried the burly owner of Figeon's. "We will raise the whole countryside; we will send a deputation to the bold Earl of Warwick; we will tell him Paul's history, and beg him to come himself, or to send a band of five hundred of his good soldiers, and destroy these bandits root and branch. If these outrages are committed in the name of the House of York, then I and mine will henceforth wear the badge of Lancaster. What we simple country folks want is a king who can keep order in this distracted land; and if that brave boy who dwelt beneath our roof, and was kindly and gracious to all, is our future king, well, God bless and keep him, say I, and let the sceptre long be held in his kindly hands!"

In the village of Much Waltham next day the wildest excitement prevailed. Jack was down at his sister's house with the dawn to tell how Paul had been rescued from the hands of the robbers the previous night, and what cruel treatment he had received at their hands. He was going off on a secret errand to the Priory that very day on Paul's behalf, to ask for news of the prince; and when it was known that the bright-haired lad (Paul's kinsman, as he had been called) who had won all hearts was none other than their future Prince of Wales, a great revulsion of feeling swept over the hearts of the simple and loving rustics, and they became as warm in their sympathies for Lancaster as they had been loyal hitherto to York.

But the burning feeling of the hour was the desire to put down by a strong hand the depredations of these lawless robber hordes. Not a house in the place but had suffered from them, not a farmer but had complaints to make of hen roost robbed or beasts driven off in the night. Others had darker tales to tell; and Will Ives clenched his fists and vowed that he would be glad indeed to see the day when he and Simon Dowsett might meet face to face in equal combat. But it would be impossible to attack the robbers in their forest fastnesses unless they had military help; and a deputation was to start forthwith to London, to lay before the mighty earl the story of the ravages committed, and the deadly peril which had just threatened the heir of England, from which he might not yet have escaped.

Jack was in hopes that he might still be at the Priory, and that he might bring him back and set him at the head of a party of loyal rustics, who should escort him in triumph to his royal father in London. But that hope was of short duration; for the news he received at the Priory told that the prince was already far away, and safe at sea on his way to France.

He had arrived just at dusk the previous evening, and when he had told his adventures and proved his identity to the satisfaction of the Prior, strenuous efforts were made to convey him safely away before further peril could menace him. It chanced that one of the brothers was about to start for

Evelyn Everett-Green

the coast on a mission for the Prior; and disguised in a friar's gown, Edward could travel with him in the most perfect safety. Stout nags were in readiness for the pair; and after the lad had been well fed, and had enjoyed a couple of hours' sleep beside the fire, he was sufficiently refreshed to proceed on his way, only charging the Prior either to send Paul after him if he should arrive in time, or to keep him in safe hiding if that should not be possible.

Before Jack left the place, the brother who had been the prince's companion returned with the news that Edward had been safely embarked in a small trading vessel bound for France, the captain of which, an ardent Lancastrian, would defend his passenger from every peril at risk of his own life if need be. The wind was favourable and light, and there was every hope of a rapid and safe passage. Before nightfall this very day Edward would probably be landed upon French soil, out of all chance of danger from foeman's steel.

As to the purposed overthrow of the robber band, the brothers most heartily approved of it. They too, though in some sort protected by the awe inspired by Holy Church, suffered from the bold dealings of these lawless men, and gladly would they see the band scattered or exterminated.

The Prior shook his head somewhat as Jack explained how he wished to wed the daughter of the chief of the crew; but when the lover pleaded his cause with all the eloquence at his command, and painted in piteous words the misery the gentle girl had endured in the midst of her unhallowed surroundings, the kind-hearted ecclesiastic relented, and forthwith despatched Brother Lawrence to examine and counsel the maid, hear her confession, and absolve her from her offences, and then, if all seemed well, to perform the rite of betrothal, which was almost as binding as the marriage service itself, and generally preceded it by a few weeks or months, as the case might be. So Jack rode off in high feather, and talked so unceasingly of his Eva the whole way to the farm, that the good brother was almost convinced beforehand of the virtue and devotion of the maid, and was willing enough a few hours later to join their hands in troth plight. After that, unless the father were prepared to draw upon himself the fulminations of the Church, he could not lay claim to his daughter, or try to give her in wedlock to another. Her place was now with her betrothed's kindred, where she would remain until the marriage ceremony itself took place, and made her indeed the daughter of the farm.

Meantime Paul lay for a while sorely sick, and was tended with motherly devotion by good Mistress Devenish, who learned to love him almost as a son. Hardy and tough as he was, the fatigue and suffering he had undergone had broken him down, and a fever set in which for a time made them fear for his very life. But his hardy constitution triumphed over the foe, and in a week's time from the night he first set foot across the threshold of Figeon's Farm he was held to be out of danger, though excessively weak and ill.

During the long nights when his hostess had watched beside him, thinking that he was either unconscious or delirious, Paul had seen and heard more than she knew. He had heard her read, as if to herself, strange and beautiful words from a book upon her knee—words that had seemed full of peace and light and comfort, and which had sunk into his weary brain with strangely soothing power. Some of these same words were not quite unfamiliar to him—at least he knew their equivalents in the Latin tongue; but somehow when spoken thus in the language of everyday life, they came home to him with tenfold greater force, whilst some of the sweetest and deepest and most comforting words were altogether new to him.

Evelyn Everett-Green

And as his strength revived, Paul's anxiety to hear more of such words grew with it; and one forenoon, as his nurse sat beside him with her busy needle flying, he looked up at her and said, "You do not read out of the book any more, and I would fain hear those wonderful words again."

"I knew not that you had ever heard."

"Yes, I heard much, and it seemed to ease my pain and give me happy thoughts. It is a beautiful and a goodly book. May I not hear more?"

"I would that all the world might hear the life giving words of that book, Paul," said the good woman with a sigh. "But they come from Wycliffe's Bible, and the holy brothers tell us that it is a wicked book, which none of us should read."

"It cannot be a wicked book which holds such goodly words—words that in the Latin tongue the Holy Church herself makes use of," said Paul stoutly. "It may be bad for unlettered and ignorant men to try to teach and expound the words they read, but the words themselves are good words. May I not see the book myself?"

"You know the risk you run in so doing, Paul?"

"Ay; but I am a good son of the Church, and I fear not to see what manner of book this be. If it is bad, I will no more of it."

The woman smiled slightly as she rose from her seat and touched a spring in the wall hard by the chimney. A sliding panel sprang back and disclosed a small shelf, upon which stood a large book, which the woman placed in Paul's hands, closing the panel immediately.

He lay still, turning the leaves with his thin hands, and

marvelling what the Church found to condemn in so holy a book as this seemed, breathing peace and goodwill and truest piety; but a slight stir without the house, and the trampling of horse hoofs in the court below, caused the woman to raise her head with an instinct of caution, and Paul to thrust the volume hastily but cautiously deep beneath the pillows on which he lay.

There were strange voices in the house, and the door was opened by Brother Lawrence, who came in with a troubled look upon his face. He was followed by three tall monks in a different habit, and with none of the rubicund joviality upon their faces that was seen in those of the brothers of Leighs Priory; whilst last of all, with a cunning and malicious leer upon his face, followed the little peddler, who, when he met the steady glance of Paul's eyes, shrank back somewhat and looked discomfited.

But the foremost of the tall monks, scarce heeding the respectful salutation made him by Paul and the mistress, turned upon the peddler and said:

"Fellow, come forward and bear your testimony. It was, you who laid the information that heretical books were hidden in this house, and that you knew the hiding place. Make good your words, now that you have brought us to the spot; for our worthy brother here speaks well of those that live beneath this roof."

"May it please your reverence, I know the place well, and that there are heretical books concealed there always. If you will press that spring in the wall here, you will see for yourself. If you find not the forbidden Bible there, call me a prating and a lying knave.",

Brother Lawrence was looking both troubled and curious,

Evelyn Everett-Green

but the face of Mistress Devenish was perfectly calm, and Paul commanded his countenance to a look of simple wonderment and surprise.

The monk obeyed the direction of the peddler; the secret spring, gave a sharp click, and the door flew open. But the little shelf was bare, and told no tales, and the face of the peddler fell.

"It has been removed—they have had notice of this visitation," stammered the discomfited man; but Brother Lawrence cut him short.

"Your reverence knows that that is impossible," he said, addressing the tall monk: "no word of this visitation had reached even our ears till your arrival this very morning. This house has ever been well thought of by our fraternity, and pays its dues to Holy Church as I would all other houses did. I trust your mind is satisfied."

The monk bent his head; but before he could speak, Paul had raised himself on his pillows, and was speaking in quick, earnest tones.

"Holy father, listen, I pray you, to me," he said, "and trust not the testimony of yon traitorous fellow, who, if he had had his will, would have done to death the son of our sainted monarch King Henry.

"Nay, let him not escape," he cried, as he saw the man make an attempt to reach the door, which was promptly frustrated by the sudden appearance of Jack Devenish, who had heard of this sudden incursion of monks, and had rushed to the house in some fear of what might be happening there.

"Hold him fast, Jack," cried Paul, with increasing energy,

"till I have told my tale;" and forthwith he described in graphic words how this man had identified the prince, and had striven to sell him to the enemy, that the House of York might triumph in his death, or in possession of the heir whose life alone could redeem the cause of Lancaster from destruction. The story was listened to with deep attention and no little sympathy, for the visit, the peril, and the flight of the prince were becoming known in this part of the country, and the clergy of all degrees were thankful indeed that the heir of England was safe, as they were all deeply attached to the cause of the Red Rose.

So Paul's story roused a great wave of anger against the mean fellow, who would thus earn his own living by betraying those whose bread he had eaten, or one whose life it should be his care to protect; and scarce had Paul done speaking before Brother Lawrence took up the gauntlet, and addressing himself to the tall monk, pointed to Paul, as he lay still white and weak upon his pillows.

"And hear farther, reverend father: this youth who now speaks to you is he of whom I told you as we rode along, who bore torture without yielding up the name of the hiding place to which he knew the prince had escaped. But for him young Edward might yet have fallen into the hands of these robbers; for they would have watched our Priory and have set upon all who went or came, and ravaged the whole country, so that even the habit of the monk would not have protected or disguised him. And these good folks here at this farm were they who rescued him from the hands of the robbers; for the maiden alone, without the help of this stalwart youth, could not have brought him, ill and fainting as he was, all these long weary miles. And they took him in; and this woman, whom yon informer would have you believe is a vile heretic, has nursed him like his own mother, and brought him back from the very jaws of death. And is

Evelyn Everett-Green

she who has done a service that royal Henry will one day thank her for publicly (for this pallid youth is as a brother in love to young Edward, and his especial charge to us till he comes again to claim him and bestow his well-earned knighthood upon him)—is she to suffer from the unproven charges of a base spy and Yorkist tool like yon fellow there, who would have betrayed his own king's son to death? Away with such a fellow from the earth, I say; and let those who have sheltered England's heir, and rescued this bold youth from worse than death—let them, I say, live in peace and honour for the service they have done their country! For I wot that when young Edward comes in his own proper state again, his first care will be for those who befriended him in his hour of need, his first chastisement against those who have done aught to harm them, if they be still cumbering the earth."

And with that the usually jovial brother, moved now by a great access of wrath, which had given him unwonted eloquence, pointed a finger significantly at the trembling peddler; and Jack, who held him by the collar, gave him a shake and said:

"Give me leave to carry him to the village green and tell the good folks there the tale, and I warrant that he will not cumber the ground much longer."

"Do with him as you will," said the tall monk, "he is no charge of mine; and if all be true that is said, he well deserves his fate."

The peddler was borne away, crying and entreating, and before an hour had passed, his dead body was hanging on an oak tree nigh to the blacksmith's forge—a warning to all informers; and when he had gone the tall monk turned to Paul with a more benign air, and laid his hand upon his head as he said:

"Thou art a stanch lad; and for their care to thee these honest folks deserve the gratitude of the Church. I believe none of the accusations of that lewd fellow. I trow this is a godly house, where the Lord is rightly honoured in His holy ordinances."

"That indeed is so," answered Paul fervently.

The visitors departed well satisfied; whilst Paul heaved a great sigh of relief, and wondered if he had in any way sinned by thought or word or deed. But his conscience was clear; he could not see that there was sin in reading holy words from God's own Book. Such matters of dispute were too hard for him, and he closed his tired eyes and was soon sound asleep. He saw the great Bible no more whilst he remained beneath that roof; but many of its words were engraved upon his heart, and were a guide to his steps and a light to his path throughout his subsequent life.

"You have saved us from a great peril this day, Paul," said the farmer that night, with a moisture in his eyes and a gravity upon his jolly face. "If we have given shelter and protection to you, your protection of us has been equally great. You must make this your home, my boy, so long as you need one."

The next days were full of excitement for Much Waltham. The request made by the people of Essex had been listened to by the great earl, and though he could scarce credit the fact that the king's son had been so near, he was convinced at last, and burned to avenge himself on those who had tried to take him captive. A band of armed men was sent down, and the forest swept clear of the marauders—at least for a while. Will Ives had his wish, and met Simon Dowsett face to face in a hand-to-hand struggle; and although the latter did all to deserve his undesirable sobriquet, he was overpowered at last and slain, and his head carried in triumph to his native village, where, after the savage custom of the day, it was exposed on a pike on the village green.

Paul heard of this fight by report alone, for he was able to get only as far as the great kitchen fire, where he and Eva spent a great part of their time in eagerly discussing the questions of the day. Her father, the chief of the band, made his escape with some few of his followers, and was heard of no more in those parts. His daughter was glad he was not killed, though she could not desire to see him more; and in a short time she and Jack were married, and she almost forgot that she had been for so many years living amongst the robbers of Black Notley.

CHAPTER 8

THE RALLY OF THE RED ROSE

"Paul! Is it really you? Now indeed I feel that I have reached my native land again. O Paul, I have wearied sorely for you. Why followed you not me to France, as we planned? Every day I looked for tidings of you, and none came. But this meeting atones for all."

It was the bright dawn of an Easter day, and Paul, after a night's hard riding, stood within the precincts of the Abbey of Cerne, not far from the seaport of Weymouth. His hands were closely grasped in those of young Edward, who was looking into his face with beaming eyes.

It was no longer the fugitive Edward of the winter months, but a royally equipped and accoutred youth, upon whose noble face and figure Paul's eyes dwelt with fond pride. Weary and tempestuous as had been the voyage from France to England—a voyage that had lasted seventeen days, in lieu of scarce so many hours—yet the bright face of the Prince of Wales bore no signs of fatigue or disappointment. The weary days of waiting were over. He and his mother had come to share his father's royal state, and drive from the shores—if he came—the bold usurper who had hitherto triumphed in the strife of the Roses. His heart beat high with hope and lofty

Evelyn Everett-Green

purpose; and in joy at the eager welcomes poured upon him by the friends and warriors who came flocking to his standard he forgot all the doubts and fears of the past, and looked upon himself as the saviour of his country, as indeed he was regarded by all his party.

The old comrades and friends looked each other well over with smiling glances, and it seemed as if Edward marked in Paul as much change in the outward man as he had done in the prince.

"By my troth, Paul, fair fortune has smiled upon you since last we met. And the gold spurs of knighthood too—nay, now, what means that, good comrade? Were we not to have knelt side by side to receive that honour? Have you outstripped me from the first?"

"Pardon, my dear lord," answered Paul, blushing and smiling; "I would sooner have received the honour at your hands than at those of any other. But I was summoned to London, so soon as my wounds were healed, by the great earl; and your royal father himself gave me audience, to ask news of you (for it became known that you had visited the realm by stealth); and after I had told him all my tale, he with his own hand bestowed that honour upon me. Then the noble earl made over to me a fair manor in the west country, which I have not yet visited, but which has put money once more into my purse. And here am I, your grace's loyal servant, to ask no better than to follow and fight for you until the crown is safely placed upon your head."

And he bent the knee and pressed his lips upon the prince's hand.

But Edward raised him, and linked his arm within that of his old companion, walking with him along the pleasant green pathway of the Abbey mead, not content till he had heard every detail of that which had befallen Paul, from the moment they had parted up till the present, and listening with intense excitement to his account of what had befallen him in the robbers' cave, and how he had escaped from thence, and had been tended and protected at Figeon's by the kindly and honest folks there.

"When I am king," said young Edward, with flashing eyes, "I will go thither again, and reward them royally for all they have done for you and me. I am glad they loved me still, Lancastrian though they knew me at last to be. Oh, if they were willing to follow my fortunes and own me as their king, methinks others will not be far behind! And, God helping me, I will try to show them what manner of man a king should be."

For it had been fully recognized upon all hands now that the prince's father was absolutely incapable of more than the name of king, and it was well known that the prince was to be the real ruler, with the name of regent, and that it would be his hands or his mother's that would sway the sceptre of power, should the Lancastrian cause triumph in the struggle.

And no thought of aught but victory had as yet found place in young Edward's heart. Was not the great invincible earl fighting on their side? And had he not already placed Henry once more upon the throne, not to be again deposed so long as he had a soldier left to fight for him?

But Paul's heart was scarce so light, although the sight of the prince awakened his loyal enthusiasm.

"O my lord, if you had but come sooner—had come before the proud son of York had landed, and drawn to his standard a host of powerful followers! I know not how it is, but his

Evelyn Everett-Green

name is a magnet that strangely stirs the hearts of men. Ere I left London I heard that the rival armies were closely approaching each other, and that the battle might not be much longer delayed. I knew not whether to fly to welcome you, or to stay and draw the sword on your behalf, and strive to be the one to bring to you the glorious news of victory. I cannot think but what the great earl will again be victorious; but the despatches he intrusted to me, with commands to hasten westwards to try and meet you on your landing, will tell you more of the chances of war than I can do. Men's mouths are full of rumours. One knows not how to sift the false from the true. But the men of London—ay, there is the peril—they all stand sullen when we of the Red Rose pass by, and scarce a voice calls 'God save the king.' If Edward of York were to succeed in reaching the city—"

"But he must not—he shall not—he cannot!" cried young Edward, with flashing eyes. "What! shall the proud crest of my great father-in-law stoop before the traitorous host of York? Fie on thee, Paul! talk not to me of defeat. Nay, after we have heard the holy mass of this glad Easter day, let us rather to horse and away—you and I together, Paul, as we have done times before—and let us not draw rein till we ride into the victorious camp of the king my father, and hear the glad welcome we shall receive from his brave host.

"O Paul, I have had my moments of doubt and desponding, but they are all past now. I come to claim my kingdom, and to place a crown upon the brow of my lovely bride. Ah, I must present you to her—my gentle Lady Anne. I wot she will not be far off She will be seeking for me, as is her fashion if we are long apart. She must thank you herself for all that you have done and suffered for me. You will feel yourself a thousandfold repaid when you have heard her sweet words of recognition."

And in effect, as they turned once more toward the Abbey, Paul saw approaching them the slight and graceful figure of a young girl, in the first blush of maiden bloom and beauty, her face ethereally lovely, yet tinged, as it seemed, with some haunting melancholy, which gave a strange pathos to its rare beauty, and seemed almost to speak of the doom of sorrow and loss already hanging over her, little as she knew it then.

The solemn troth plight which had passed between her and young Edward was almost equivalent to the marriage vow that would shortly bind them indissolubly together, and their love for each other was already that of man and wife. As the gentle lady listened to the eager tale poured out by Paul, she stretched out her hand to him, and when he would have bent the knee she raised him up with sweet smiles, and told him how her dear lord had always praised him as a very brother, and the type of all that was faithful and true in comrade. Such words from such lips brought the boyish blush to Paul's cheeks, and he stumbled bashfully over his undying protestations of loyalty.

Then, as they reached the refectory, which had been allotted by the monks to their noble guests, he stopped short and fell upon his knees; for in a tall and stately figure advancing to meet them he recognized the great queen he had not seen since he was a child, and scarce dared to raise his eyes to note the ravages that sorrow and care had made upon that princely visage, or the silver whiteness of the locks, covered for the most part by the tall, peaked headdress of the day.

The queen recognized Paul at once from the strange likeness to her own son, and her welcome was kindly given. But she was anxious and preoccupied, having but risen from the perusal of the despatches Paul had brought; and although her natural courage and hopefulness would not permit her to

Evelyn Everett-Green

despond, she could not but admit that danger menaced the cause of the Red Rose, whilst she realized, as her young son could not do at his age, how utterly disastrous would be a single victory of the enemy at such a juncture.

The fortunes of the rival houses were trembling in the balance. The first decisive, advantage to either would give a prestige and fillip to that cause which might be absolutely fatal to the hopes of the other. If it were true that some battle were being fought or about to be fought that very day, such a battle might be either the death blow to all their hopes or the earnest of a final triumph nigh at hand.

It was a strange Easter Day for the party at the Abbey. The mass was quickly followed by the arrival of loyal adherents from the surrounding country, who had heard of the landing of the long-expected party from France, and flocked eagerly to pay their homage to the queen and the prince, and look upon the fair face of the Lady Anne, whose position as Warwick's daughter and Edward's bride alike made her an object of the greatest interest and a person of importance. Paul was deeply enamoured of the gentle and lovely lady, and received many marks of favour from her hands. He was given a post about the young prince, and kept close at his side the whole day.

It was inspiriting indeed to hear the loyal protestations of the friends who kept flocking all day to join their standard, and there was no riding forth to London for prince or attendant so long as the light lasted.

"But tomorrow morn we will sally forth ere it well be day," said Edward, in low tones, as they parted for the night. "My heart tells me that something of note has occurred this very day. We will be the first to bring the news to my mother. Be ready with a couple of horses and some few men-at-arms ere the sun be well risen over yon ridge, and we will forth to meet the messengers of victory, and bring them back with us to tell their welcome news."

Paul had forgotten his vague fears in the gladness of the present, and scarce closed his eyes that night, thinking of the coming triumph for the prince he loyally loved. He was up and in the saddle with the first glimmering light of day, and by the time that the rosy glow of dawn was transforming the fair world of nature and clothing it with an indescribable radiance of gossamer beauty, he and the prince were already a mile from the Abbey, galloping along in the fresh morning air with a glad exultation of spirit that seemed in itself like a herald of coming triumph.

"The very heavens have put on the livery of the Red Rose!" cried Edward gaily, as he pointed to the vivid red of the east; and Paul smiled, and tried to banish from his mind the old adage learned at his nurse's knee, to the effect that a red morn was the herald of a dark and dreary day.

They had ridden a matter of some five miles forth in the direction of the great road to London—as it was then considered, though we should scarce call the rude tracks of those days roads—when the quick eye of Paul caught sight of a little moving cloud of dust, and he drew rein to shade his eyes with his hand.

Edward followed his example, and together they stood gazing, their hearts beating with sympathetic excitement. How much might the next few moments contain for them of triumph or of despair! for from the haste with which these horsemen rode, it was plain they were the bearers of tidings, and if of tidings, most likely those of some battle, in which the King Maker and the king he had first made and then driven away would stand for the first time in hostile ranks.

Evelyn Everett-Green

Together they had been victorious; what would be the result when they met as foes?

Nearer and nearer came the riders, looming through the uncertain morning mist, and emerging thence two jaded, weary figures, their horses flecked with foam, nostrils wide, chests heaving, showing every sign of distress; and Paul, recognizing in one of the riders a follower of the Earl of Warwick, called upon him by name, and bid him speak his tidings.

"Lost—lost—all lost!" cried the man, addressing himself to Paul, unconscious of the identity of his companion; "the battle is fought and lost. The armies met on Barnet Heath. The Earl of Warwick, the great earl, was there slain. His Majesty King Henry is again a prisoner in the hands of Edward of York. Today he makes his triumphant entry into London, which will open its gates to him with joy and receive him as king."

Paul sat rigid and motionless as he heard these words. He did not dare to look at young Edward, who sat beside him as if turned to stone. The second messenger, who had had a moment to draw breath whilst his fellow had been speaking, now broke in with his share of the terrible news. He had seen the prodigies of valour performed by the mighty earl. He had witnessed the death of that warrior—such a death as was fitting for one of his warlike race. The testimony of eyewitnesses could not be doubted. The fatal day had again been hostile to the cause of the Red Rose, and the mournful cry of those who had seen and shared in the fight, as they fled pellmell from the field, had been, "Lost—all lost! the House of Lancaster is utterly overthrown!"

Mournfully the little procession turned itself and rode back to the Abbey. Edward had not spoken one word all this time, and the messengers, who had now learned who he was, fell to the rear, and observed an awed silence. But their tale had been told. They had said enough. The worst was made known, and not even Paul dared venture a word of consolation, or seek to know what was passing in the mind of the prince, whose fair inheritance seemed thus to be slipping away.

Excitement, uncertainty, and suspense seemed in the very air, and even before the silent little troop reached the courtyard of the Abbey eager forms were seen hurrying out, and the tall and stately figure of the royal Margaret stood outlined in the doorway. Perhaps something in the very silence and confused looks of the little group told a tale of disaster, for the queen came hurrying down the steps with whitening face, and her son sprang from his saddle and put his arm about her, as if to support her in the shock which could not but fall upon her now.

"Tell me all," she whispered hoarsely. "Do not keep me in suspense. Speak, I command you, my son."

"A battle has been fought—and lost," answered Edward, speaking mechanically. "Our ally and friend the Earl of Warwick was killed in desperate fight. My father is a prisoner in the enemy's hands. Edward of York is even now making his triumphant entry into London, which will receive him with open arms."

Edward said no more; he had indeed told all his tale, and it had been enough for the unhappy woman, who had landed on English soil so confident of victory. She gave one short, low cry, a convulsive shudder passed through her limbs, and she fell senseless to the ground. That cry found its echo upon the pale lips of another—one who had closely followed the queen to learn the tidings of the travellers; and Edward

Evelyn Everett-Green

turned to catch his bride in his arms, whilst her tears rained down fast as she heard how her noble father lay dead upon the fatal field that had lost her lord his crown, and had dashed to the ground the warmest hopes of the Red Rose.

"Let us to ship again," said Margaret, as she recovered from her long swoon. "The cause is lost without hope. Warwick is slain. Whom have we now to trust to? Let us back to France, and hide our dishonoured heads there. My father's court will receive us yet, and perchance we may in time learn to forget that we were ever princes and sovereigns."

Strange words, indeed, from the haughty and warlike Margaret; but at that moment her proud spirit seemed crushed and broken, and it was young Edward who answered her with words of hope and courage.

"Nay, mother," he said, "let it not be said of the House of Plantagenet that they turned their backs upon the foe, and fled disgracefully, leaving their followers to butchery and ruin. It might have been well for us never to have disturbed again the peace of this realm; but having summoned to our banner the loyal adherents of the Red Rose, it is not for us to fly to safety, and leave them to the wrath and cruelty of Edward. No; one battle—one defeat—does not lose us our cause. My father lives; shall we leave him to linger out his days in hopeless captivity? I live; have I not the right to strike a blow for the crown to which I was born?

"Courage, sweet mother. You are a king's daughter. You have led men to victory before. Say not—think not—that all is lost. Let us win the crown of England by the power of the name and of the righteous cause we own, and henceforth shall no man say that a subject crowns and dethrones England's monarch at his will."

These words, seconded and echoed by those of many a gallant knight and noble, raised Margaret's broken spirit, and she began once more to hope. That day they journeyed by rapid stages to Beaulieu Abbey, a very famous sanctuary in those days, the ruins of which may still be seen in the New Forest; and there the party found the widowed Countess of Warwick, who had landed at Portsmouth before the royal party had reached Weymouth, and had just heard of her terrible loss. To have her daughter with her once again, and to mingle their tears together, was some consolation, both for the countess and the Lady Anne; but others had sterner work before them than weeping over past misfortunes, and as soon as the retreat of the royal Lancastrian became generally known, many stanch adherents flocked to tender their allegiance and promise fealty to the cause.

Foremost amongst these was the young Duke of Somerset, whose family had ever been stanch to the Red Rose, as well it might. Some of the unpopularity Margaret of Anjou had early won for herself at the English court was due to her confidence in and affection for Somerset, and his son might well be ardent in her cause.

Margaret herself was still sunk in unwonted depression, but the representations of the fiery young duke did much to give her heart. With him came Jasper Tudor, the king's half brother, and they drew glowing pictures of the loyalty of the western counties; and of Wales, where a large band of troops was mustering for her support; and represented that if she could but effect a junction with them, the whole country would soon be hers, and she would be able to dictate terms to the enemy at the gates of London.

Margaret's elastic temper rose with the encouragement thus received, and Edward's heart beat high with hope. The party began their westward march, and through the bright days of

Evelyn Everett-Green

April and May they rode through the smiling land, receiving welcome and adulation from all, and reinforcements to their little band from every town through which they passed. Small wonder was it that they learned to feel confident of ultimate success. The young prince, with Paul at his side, would ride through the ranks of his followers day by day, speaking bright, brave words to all he passed, and winning the hearts of his troops as perhaps only the young and frank-hearted and unspoiled can do. To him it seemed almost more like a triumphal progress than a recruiting march.

But Margaret's brow was often dark with anxiety. She knew the temper of the bold Edward of York, as she called him, whom the world still spoke of as king; and she knew that he would be upon their track. Any day they might see his banners threatening their rear, and still the Welsh army was at some distance; and until a junction could be effected, even their lives could scarce be called safe.

Then at Gloucester a serious check met them. The place was held for the king's brother, and the gates were resolutely closed against her. It was here that she had reckoned upon crossing the deep and treacherous waters of the Severn, and to be thus foiled might mean the ruin of the enterprise. The sheltering mountains of Wales were already in sight; but how was she to reach them if the passage of the river were denied her?

Paul had gone forth alone that day, and had not been present when the queen had ridden herself to the fortified gates to demand an entrance, which had been firmly and respectfully declined her. But he had learned tidings which disquieted him not a little, and it was at full gallop that he dashed back into the ranks, and sought the prince himself, who was looking with darkening brow upon the frowning battlements of the unfriendly city.

"My liege, it brooks not this delay," he cried, reining up beside Edward, and speaking in rapid whispers. "The army of York is scarce a score of miles away, and in hot pursuit after us. They have had certain news of our movements, and unless we can push on across the river and meet our friends there, we shall be taken in the rear, and at sore disadvantage. It behoves us to strain every nerve to reach our friends before our foes are upon us."

"I doubt not that," answered Edward calmly, yet with a look which Paul did not understand; "but the wide river runs before us, and the bridge is barred to us. Unless we reduce first this noble city, we must turn and face the foe and fight him at sore odds."

A look of dismay crossed Paul's face as he heard this piece of news, and he silently followed the prince at his bidding to the spot where the leading nobles and generals were gathered together in warm debate. The news that Edward was just upon them ran like wildfire through the ranks, and all the most experienced leaders, including the royal Margaret herself, were of opinion that it would be better not to run the risk of a battle, but retire rapidly and stealthily from their present position, and not encounter the onset of Edward's veteran troops, flushed with victory and thirsting for blood, until their hardy mountain allies had contrived to join them.

But there is something revolting to young and ardent spirits in the thought of flight, and the Duke of Somerset was eager for the fray. He argued that an easy victory must be theirs if they did but act boldly and hastened to the attack. To fly were fatal; their troops would become disheartened and melt away. Their foes would openly triumph, and all men would be drawn to them. Edward's soldiers, weary with long marching, would be taken by surprise. It were a thousand times better to risk the fight than to play the coward at so

Evelyn Everett-Green

critical a juncture.

And these impetuous words carried the younger spirits along with them. The prince drew his sword, and riding through the ranks, asked if the soldiers would choose to fight or fly. There could scarce be more than one reply to such an appeal so made. They drew their swords and vowed to live or die with him, and the enthusiasm of the moment was such that all were carried away; and orders were instantly given for a march upon Tewkesbury, where it was thought a spot might be found which would give them advantages for the coming struggle.

The troops had had a long march earlier in the day, but they traversed the ten miles which lay between them and Tewkesbury with cheerful alacrity. Paul and the prince rode side by side in the van of the advancing host, and Edward looked straight before him with glowing eyes, as if he felt that a crisis of his fate were at hand.

"At last, my good Paul, we are riding forth to try conclusions with the world, as we have purposed so long to do," he said, with a strange, flashing smile. "In faith I am glad that the hour of action is come. Ere another sun is set some blow shall have been struck which shall set the crown of England upon some one head more firmly than ever it has been set before. God grant the cause of right may triumph! But whichever way the conflict goes, I pray that this distracted land may find peace and rest, and that I may be either a victor in the strife, or may find a soldier's grave. Paul, will you give me your promise, trusty comrade, that ere I fall alive into the hand of the foe, you will bury your knightly sword in my heart yourself? It were the part of a true brother to save me from the fate of my patient father. He has borne dethronement and captivity; but methinks I should pine and die, and I would far rather—"

He gave Paul an expressive glance; but the young knight answered gravely and steadfastly:

"My liege, ask me not that beyond my power to grant. We may not without sin raise our hands against the Lord's anointed, and I may not do the thing you ask. Death or captivity I will gladly share with you, or spend every drop of my blood to save you; but more than this no loyal knight may promise. Forgive me, my liege, if I offend in this."

But Edward held out his mailed hand with his own bright, sweet smile, grasping that of Paul, which he held in his own as he spoke.

"You are in the right, Paul, you are in the right. Perchance it were a coward thought; for should not a prince be ready for any blow of adverse fortune? But ride you into the battle beside me. Let us fight side by side, even as we have always hoped to do. I would that you were in very truth my brother, as in love you have long been. And if I fall whilst you escape, be it your office to break the tidings to my mother and my gentle Anne; for methinks, were it told them suddenly or untenderly, their hearts would break with the sorrow."

Paul gave this pledge willingly, though it scarce seemed possible to him that he should live to carry such tidings, seeing he would die a thousand deaths to save his prince from the foeman's steel. And then, with grave faces but brave hearts and unclouded brows, the comrades rode side by side into the town of Tewkesbury, whilst the army intrenched itself on the summit of a small eminence called the Home Ground, not half a mile away.

Already the rival army was mustering, and the Yorkist troops occupied the sloping ground to the south, that went by the

Evelyn Everett-Green

name of the Red Piece. The Lancastrians had the best of the situation, as they were established amongst trenches and ditches, partly real and partly artificial; which would render any attack by the enemy difficult and dangerous.

"I trow it would be hard to drive from this ground these brave men thus posted," said Edward to Paul, as the two rode round the camp at the close of the day. "They have only to stand firm and hold their position, and all will be well. Oh that the night were past, and that a new day had come! I would I could see the end of this struggle. I would the veil of the future might be for one moment lifted."

But the future keeps its secrets well—well for us it is so—and the youthful and high-spirited young prince saw not the black cloud hanging already upon him. The soldiers greeted him with cheers and blessings; the generals bent the knee to him, and vowed to die to win him back his crown. The light of the setting sun illumined the field so soon to be red with human blood, and the vesper bell from the church hard by rang out its peaceful summons.

Edward looked round him, and laid his hand affectionately on Paul's shoulder.

"This is a fair earth," he said dreamily. "I wonder what the world beyond will be like, for those who leave this behind, as so many will do tomorrow."

Paul spoke not a word, but returned the look with one infinitely loving, and together the two rode back to the town.

CHAPTER 9

THE TRAGEDY OF TEWKESBURY

How the battle of Tewkesbury was lost and won is too well known to need description in detail here. Whether the Lancastrian army could have held the field before the Yorkist veterans had they been skilfully generalled will never now be known; but the fiery and impetuous Duke of Somerset, whose ill-judged ardour had forced the battle upon his followers, undoubtedly lost the day for them by his intemperate and reckless disregard of the dictates of common prudence. After opening the fight by a discharge of ordnance, he was mad enough to leave his intrenched position on the Home Ground, and carry his men into the open for a charge upon the opposing army. Here they were not only confronted by Edward's compact army, but were taken in the flank and rear by a company of spearmen who had been told off to guard against a possible ambush in a little wood; which, however, the hot-headed Somerset had never thought to place.

Thrown into confusion, the Lancastrians were routed, and confusion was rendered worse confounded by another impetuous act on the part of the fiery young duke. As he and his flying soldiers fell back upon the town of Tewkesbury, and reached the market place, they found Lord Wenlock and

Evelyn Everett-Green

his men sitting idle and motionless there, as if there was no work for them to do.

The reason for this extraordinary apathy on the part of one of the leaders will never now be known. It was the curse of the strife of the Roses that treachery and a change of sides was always suspected, and too often with good cause, between men who had been friends and allies heretofore. The Duke of Somerset at once concluded that Lord Wenlock had turned traitor to the cause, and riding furiously up to him as he sat, he dashed out his brains with his battle-axe, without so much as pausing to ask a single question.

The followers of both leaders who saw the deed were struck with new terror. With loud cries of "Treason, treason!" they threw down their arms and fled they knew not whither, and the retreat became a confused rout, in which the thought of each man was to save his own life.

Such, in brief, was the deplorable story of the battle of Tewkesbury. But we are concerned less with the main course of the fortunes of the day than with the individual adventures of certain persons concerned, who, if isolated acts of gallantry and devotion could have saved the day, would have turned the fortunes of even the fatal field of Tewkesbury.

The prince was stationed in the main body of the army, under the care, as was supposed by his anxious mother, of the military Prior of St. John's Longstruther. And by his side was his faithful shadow, Paul, whose solemn purpose that day was to keep beside the prince throughout the course of the battle, and shield him from harm even at the cost of his own life. Some strange foreboding had fallen upon Paul, and he scarce expected to see the light of another day; but this presentiment of coming ill he bravely hid from his companion, and the two rode into the ranks with smiling faces, and looked across at the opposing lines of the enemy with a steadfast and lofty courage. Then the prince turned to his companion.

"Our first battle, good Paul; for though as a child I saw fighting, I never took part in it before. I am glad that we ride side by side this day. Let us show our loyal people, whatever be the fortunes of the field, that Englishmen can strike hard blows, and that they never turn their backs upon the foe. If we ride not to victory, Paul, let us ride to death with a courage that shall not disgrace the kingly blood that both of us can boast in some measure."

Then they looked to their weapons, and sat very silent, waiting what would befall.

Perhaps those that take part in a fierce fight know less about the details than any others. Paul was presently aware that he and the men about him, the prince still at his side, were charging down the little eminence upon which they had been posted, straight at the serried ranks of the Yorkist army, which kept its position, and awaited their coming with cool intrepidity. Paul had not time to think or reason, or he would surely have wondered at the rashness of quitting an advantageous position, and putting themselves to such disadvantage before the foe. All he knew was that the duke's company had moved first, and had charged upon the enemy, and that their military monk had given the word to follow and support their friends; which was done without a moment's hesitation, whether the movement were, strategically speaking, right or wrong.

And then, all in a moment as it seemed, the prince and his comrade found themselves in a fierce melee, in which for a while they could scarce move hand or foot, jammed in by the press of men and steeds, but surrounded by friends and comrades, who were eagerly pressing forward toward the foe. Cries and shouts rent the air, mingled sometimes with the shriek or groan which told that a well-directed blow had gone home to its mark. The press became denser, and then less dense; some riderless horses from the front rank came tearing back through the crush, forcing their way in a sort of mad terror; and Edward, snatching his battle-axe from its resting place across his saddle bow, swung it over his head, and shouted to his companion:

"Follow me, Paul! yonder lies the foe. I will strike a blow for my father's liberty and crown this day, whether I live or die."

The way was open now, and Paul saw plainly that they were close to the ranks of the foe. But there was no drawing back, even had he wished it; his blood was up now, and not even fear for the possible peril of the prince could withhold him from the charge. He knew not whether the person of the prince was known, and whether young Edward ran any especial danger in thus flinging himself upon the enemy. But it was no longer his place to think—the moment for action had arrived; and following Edward's example, he dashed into the thick of the fray, the impetuosity and fury of his charge bearing down all before him, and hewing down man and horse as he clave a passage through the ranks for the prince, who closely followed.

They were not alone. A gallant little company was following in their track, and with cries of "An Edward, an Edward, a Prince of Wales!" smote down the rival warriors with a fury which for the moment nothing could withstand. There is surely something magnetic in a war cry or in a patriotic song, for it inspires those who use it with an ardour and a strength which for the moment seem invincible.

To Paul and the prince it seemed as if the day were all but

won. Wherever they turned they dealt death and destruction. The wing of the army upon which they charged was wavering and disorganized; the infantry recoiled before the fierce charge of the horsemen, and the opposing cavalry was mostly in another part of the field.

"Victory, victory!" shouted those about Paul and the prince; and to the enthusiastic and excited lads it seemed as if the day was already theirs. The name of the Prince of Wales was in all mouths. It was shouted by each soldier as he fell upon his foe, and the enemy appeared to recoil before it. Onward and ever onward pressed the eager little band, until it was entirely separated from the main body of the army; and so certain were all who took part in that isolated skirmish that the fortunes of the day were with the House of Lancaster, that the peril of their position struck none of the prince's followers till, thinned by the blows of their adversaries, and weary with the impetuosity of their own charge, they paused and drew together; whilst the foe, glad of a moment's breathing space, did not molest them.

There are pauses even on the battlefield when a few words can be exchanged, and the prince, flushed with the foretaste (as it seemed to him) of a glorious victory, turned to Paul with kindling eyes.

"War is a glorious game in all truth, Paul. I would not have been elsewhere for all the world. But you bleed—you are wounded. Tell me where. I knew not that you were hurt. You must ride back to the town and be tended there."

"Nay, it is nought; I do not even feel it. I know not who struck me, nor when. I will bind this scarf about my arm, and all will be well. And think you not, my liege, that it were well to return to the lines ourselves? I promised your royal mother and the Lady Anne that you should not adventure

Evelyn Everett-Green

yourself too much today within the enemy's lines. But all such charge passed from my memory in the heat of the fight."

"Ay, and my place was here, in the midst of my good soldiers. Oh, it has been a glorious day! 'Lancaster will remember it ever. And see, Paul—see how they fly on yonder height! See how the battle rages and becomes a flight! It is the same everywhere. The Red Rose triumphs. Proud York is forced to fly. Shall we join them, and lead again to victory? They are chasing them to the very walls of the town."

Paul looked in the direction indicated, and a change came over his face. He had the wonderful long, keen sight which often comes to those who have grown up in the open air, and have been used from childhood to the exercise of hunting and hawking. The prince saw only the flying rout, which he concluded to be the soldiers of York; but Paul could distinguish more. He could see the colours, and the badges they wore, and he recognized with a sinking heart the terrible fact that it was the followers of the Red Rose who were flying before the mailed warriors of Edward of York.

The change in his countenance did not escape young Edward's keen eye, and he at once divined the cause, The bright flush faded from his own face, and his gaze was turned in the same direction again.

Alas! it was but too plain now; for the rout was plainly in the direction of the town, and it was easy to understand that had it been the Yorkists who had fled they would have taken an opposite direction, in order to reach their own lines.

For a moment prince and subject sat spellbound, watching that terrible sight in deep silence. But then the peril of their own position, and the deadly danger that menaced the prince if the situation should be realized by their foes surrounding them here, flashed across Paul like a vivid and terrible lightning gleam.

He turned and laid his hand upon the shoulder of the prince.

"My liege," he said, "we may not linger here. We must regain our comrades, and see if we may rally them yet. All may not be lost, but it were madness to remain here. Let me call our followers together, and we will charge back through the foe to our own lines. It is not safe to be here."

Edward made no reply. The face that had been flushed with victory and bright with hope was now set in those stern lines which seem to speak of a forlorn hope. He saw their peril as clearly as Paul; but if the day were lost, what mattered it if his life were yet whole in him? The face he silently turned upon his companion seemed to have grown years older whilst he had been speaking.

And to make matters worse, the knowledge of the disaster to their own side spread to the soldiers who had followed the prince, and that instant demoralization which so often accompanies and aggravates defeat seized upon the men. They flung away their heavier arms, and with a shout of "Treason, treason!"—for they were assured there had been foul play somewhere—fled each man by himself, without a thought for aught save his own life.

Paul and the prince thus found themselves alone in the midst of a hostile host—alone save for the presence of some half-dozen stout troopers attached to the service of Paul, who since his advance in worldly prosperity had been in a position to engage and retain the services of some men-at-arms of his own. These faithful fellows, who had learned to love their

Evelyn Everett-Green

young master, sat doggedly in their saddles, prepared to sell their lives dear, and to carry off if possible their master and the prince living from the field. But they, too, realized how desperate was the situation; and the threatening and triumphant glances of their enemies, who now began to close up round them, showed that others had realized that the battle was already won by the Yorkist faction.

"King Edward, King Edward!" shouted the fierce soldiers as they grasped their weapons anew. "Down with the Red Rose! Down with all false princes! Down with the traitors who would disturb the peace of the land! King Edward, King Edward!"

The prince looked at Paul, and Paul looked at the prince. The same thought was in the minds of both.

"We will at least sell our lives dear," said young Edward in low tones. "My trusty comrade, your loyalty to the Red Rose has been but a sorry thing for you. I would I could have rewarded you with such honours as a prince has to give; but—"

"It is honour enough for me, my liege, to die at your side—to die, if it may be, in saving your life," said Paul. "Talk not so, I beseech you. The happiness of my life has been in calling myself your servant. It will be a happy death that is died at your side."

"Not servant—comrade, friend, brother," said Ed ward, holding out his hand once again, with a look that Paul never forgot. "No more, Paul. I must play the man; and such words go deep, and bring the tears to mine eyes. Paul, there are strange chances in battle, and it may be that you will live through it, and that I may be slain: If such be so, tell my mother and my wife (for she is that to me, as I am her husband in love) that I died as a prince of the House of Plantagenet should do—sword in hand and face to the foe. Tell my mother that such a death is better than an inglorious life of exile, and bid her not weep for me. There is yet another world than this in which we shall meet, where the strife of war is not heard and the malice of foes pursues us not. Let her look forward to our meeting there. It were a better prospect, in all truth, than an earthly crown, which methinks sits heavy on the head of him that wears it."

Paul said nothing, for he could not trust himself to speak, and indeed the brief respite was at an end. With loud and threatening cries the foe was closing round the devoted little band, and from the other side of the field he could see that a knot of horsemen were galloping in their direction, as though they had got some news of the presence of the prince.

Wounded as he was, and spent from having borne the brunt of that first gallant charge, Paul yet set his teeth and nerved himself for a last desperate rally. If they could cut their way through the ranks of the foes and gain the town, they might be safe at least for the moment; and that was the object of himself and his servants. Placing the reluctant prince in the midst, so as if possible to save at least him from steel or lead, the gallant little band with axes and pikes commenced hewing its way through the living wall which surrounded it. And so gallantly did the good steeds respond to the urging of their riders, and so fierce were the blows that rained down upon the heads of the footmen who barred their passage, that for a moment it seemed as if they would yet win their way back, and gain the protection of such of their comrades as had not shared in the general rout.

But alas! though the footmen gave way before them, the mounted soldiers, who were speeding across the field, saw at once the line they were taking, and galloped headlong to

Evelyn Everett-Green

intercept them. Paul, in the fury of his hot young blood, dashed forward alone, and fell upon the foremost with so fierce a blow that his axe was wedged in the head-piece of his opponent, so that he was unable to draw it out. The man reeled in his saddle and fell, almost dragging Paul, who still had hold of the axe, with him; and before he could recover himself or draw his sword, he was set upon by half a score mounted riders.

For one moment he was aware of merciless blows raining down upon him, battering him to the earth; he felt suffocated, crushed, more utterly helpless and powerless than he had ever done in his life before. Quick thrills of pain were running through him, stars danced before his eyes; and through all this confusion and distress he was yet aware of some terrible danger menacing the prince—danger from which he had sworn to save him at the risk of his own life. He struggled fiercely and blindly with the foes who seemed to be above and about him, knocking the wind from his body, and holding his throat in an iron clasp. Consciousness was fast deserting him. The dancing stars had disappeared, leaving the blackest darkness behind them. He made one frantic effort to break the chain which seemed to be grinding his very life out of him, and then followed a space of blankness that must surely have been like death itself.

It might have been minutes, hours, days, or even years before Paul opened his eyes to the light of day once more, for all consciousness he had of the flight of time; but when he did so it was to meet the solicitous glance of a pair of friendly eyes, and to feel himself supported by strong arms, whilst some potent spirit was held to his lips, which, when he had drunk of it, seemed to drive away the mists and give him back his senses again.

He looked round him, and found himself lying upon a bloody

field, dead and wounded strewn about him. He was upheld by the arm of one of his own stout servants; and no one else save a few wounded men or dead corpses was near. In a flash it all came back—the fight, the supposed victory, the disastrous defeat; and he groaned aloud, and struggled to regain his feet.

"The prince!" he cried, in tones sharpened by physical and mental anguish, "the prince!—where is he?"

"He is a prisoner; but he is unhurt. A gallant knight took him. His name, I learned from one of his men-at-arms, is Sir Richard Crofts; and he called out to his men, after you were down, that he would have no hurt done to the prince. He was to be taken prisoner and brought to the king—so he called him; and he had given out by proclamation that whoever brought to him the prince, alive or dead, should have a hundred pounds a year; and that the life of the prince should be spared. This I learned from the man-at-arms who stayed behind with me a while, to bind up a wound you had given him, and to help me to unlace your helmet, which was going nigh to choke you as you lay.

"Fear not for the prince, good master. His life is safe; and doubtless his noble aspect will win him favour with him they now call king."

"Nay, why do you struggle with me? you can scarce stand yet. Whither would you go? Let me catch some riderless steed and carry you to the town. Methinks the leaders have taken sanctuary with the queen in the church. You had better join them there."

"Ay, get me a horse," said Paul, with faint but vehement command; and he leaned heavily upon his sword as his servant departed to do his bidding.

Evelyn Everett-Green

Battered, sore wounded as he felt himself to be, instinct told him that he could act now as it would be impossible to do later, when his wounds began to stiffen and his muscles to refuse to obey his will. No bones were broken. He could still keep his feet and use his arms; and when the faithful servant brought up a horse and helped his master to mount, Paul felt that giddy and weak and suffering as he was, he could yet make shift to ride as far as it would be needful to do. The royal pennon floating over a certain tent not so very far away told him that his goal might yet be reached before his strength deserted him. The fiery spirit of which he again partook gave him temporary power. He scarce knew what he wished to do, save that he must stand beside his prince when he was brought to Edward's presence, and if harm befell him there, share it with him, as he had shared his peril that fatal day.

"Save yourself, good Adam," he said to his servant when he was once mounted; "I am going to follow the prince. But come not near the enemy's lines yourself, lest mischief befall you."

And before the astonished servant could speak a word of remonstrance, Paul had set spurs to his horse and had galloped off in the direction of the enemy's camp.

Within the lines there was the confusion incident to a battle, and no one heeded the battered rider, who, his helmet left behind and his mail dinted and disfigured by the hard blows it had received, had nothing about him to show to which army he belonged. Soldiers were leaning on their swords and eagerly discussing the fortunes of the day; and round and about Edward's royal tent a dense crowd had gathered, out of curiosity, it was said—and Paul heard the words—to see what manner of reception would be met at the monarch's hands by the youthful Edward, called "Prince," who had been brought into the lines by Sir Richard Crofts.

The proclamation respecting him was widely known throughout the camp, and it was said on all hands that the life of the prince would be safe; but whether he would share his father's captivity or be banished the kingdom with his French mother were points no one could answer.

And Paul rode silently and swiftly by, glad that no one heeded him or challenged him to give an account of himself.

Dismounting at last as he reached the outskirts of the crowd, and turning his horse loose to find its own master if it could, Paul was about to push his way into the eager knot of spectators, when a hand was laid upon his arm; and turning suddenly, he found himself confronted by a delicate page boy, whose white face and dilated eyes seemed to bespeak the extreme of emotion and distress. Before he had time to speak or to ask a question, the page addressed him; and as soon as the voice smote upon his ears Paul started and turned even paler than he had been; for he had heard those musical tones before, and in the fair page before him he recognized, to his horror and dismay, the gentle Lady Anne—young Edward's bride—here, alone and unprotected, in the heart of the foe's camp.

She saw that she was recognized, and laid her hand upon her lips in token of silence. Paul choked back the words that were upon his tongue, and looked at her in mute amaze.

"I could not keep away," she whispered, "when they told me all was lost and he had not returned. It was the only way. No one has heeded me in the tumult and strife. I heard all. I heard he was prisoner—that he was to be brought before Edward of York. Paul, I knew that you would be near him. I knew, if living, I should find you. See, they heed us not. They care not whether we be friends or foes. Take me through the crowd; take me to him. I am safe with you. Let

Evelyn Everett-Green

us all die together."

Paul, utterly bewildered and astonished by this extraordinary meeting, could only obey in silence. It was all like some hideous, oppressive dream. Little by little he and his companion made their way through the throng until they reached the line of armed sentries who kept their stations outside the royal tent. Here they would have had to pause, had not Paul made a step forward and said boldly:

"I am the servant squire of the prisoner, and I claim the right to stand at his side and share his fate, whatever it may be. Let me and this lad, I pray you, go to him. We desire nothing better than to lay down our lives with him."

The sentries eyed the pair doubtfully. Their unarmed condition and Paul's visibly battered state told that these were no dangerous conspirators; and devotion to a lost cause always stirs the generous feelings of brave men. It may, however, be doubted whether the pair would have gained their wish had it not been for the fact that at this moment Edward himself appeared, disarmed, but otherwise treated with due honour and courtesy, attended by his captor, who was leading him to the king's tent in obedience to a summons just received.

The moment that she saw her betrothed husband, no power on earth would have been strong enough to hold back the fair-faced page, under whose boyish dress a faithful woman's heart was beating. The disguised maiden sprang forward and sank at the feet of her supposed master, seizing his hand and covering it with kisses as she tenderly murmured his name.

Edward instantly recognized her—Paul saw that at once; but the shock of the discovery steadied his nerves, as he realized the peril in which she had placed herself, and he looked round for one who might save her when he himself might be powerless to do so. It was at that moment—as the crowd stood speechless, touched and perplexed by the little scene, and reluctant to rough-handle so fair a boy, and one whose devotion was so bravely displayed—that Paul took occasion to step forward and present himself before Edward.

A look of relief instantly crossed the prince's face.

"I might have known that you would have been here—ever nearest in the hour of deadliest peril. Paul, whatever befalls me, take care of him." Low as the words were spoken, the prince dared not use the other pronoun. "Keep him safe. Take him to my mother; she will protect him from the menaced peril."

"I will, my liege, I will," said Paul; and it was he who raised the form of the trembling page, and together the three were pushed not ungently into the royal presence—Sir Richard being a man of kindly nature, and having been touched by the devotion evinced by these two youths (as he supposed them) in braving the dangers of the camp in order to be with their prince when he was called upon to answer for his life before the offended monarch.

Edward was standing in his tent, surrounded by his nobles, brothers, and his wife's kinsmen, as the young Plantagenet prince was brought before him. Perhaps England hardly possessed a finer man than its present king, who was taller by the head than almost any of those who stood round him, his dress of mail adding to the dignity of his mien, and his handsome but deeply-lined features, now set in stern displeasure, showing at once the indications of an unusual beauty and a proud and relentless nature.

The youthful Edward was brought a few paces forward by

Evelyn Everett-Green

the attendants; whilst Paul stood in the background, longing to be beside his prince, but obliged to support the trembling form of Anne, who had been his liege's last charge to him.

"Is this the stripling they falsely call the Prince of Wales?" quoth Edward, stepping one pace nearer and regarding the noble lad with haughty displeasure. "How dost thou dare to come thus presumptuously to my realms with banners displayed against me?"

"To recover my father's kingdom and mine own inheritance," was the bold but unhesitating answer of the kingly youth, who, fettered and prisoner as he was, had all the fearless Plantagenet blood running in his veins.

The eagle eye of Edward flashed ominously, and making one more step toward his unarmed prisoner, he struck him in the face with his iron gauntlet. In a moment a dozen swords flashed from their scabbards. It seemed as if the bloodthirsty nobles awaited but this signal for the ruthless attack upon the deposed monarch's son which has left so dark a stain upon one page of history.

Paul, all unarmed as he was, would have sprung forward to die with his prince, but was impeded by the senseless burden now lying a dead weight in his arms. At the king's blow the page had uttered a faint cry; and as the first of those murderous weapons were plunged in the breast of her youthful lover, she fell to the earth like a stone, or would have done, but that Paul flung his arm about her, and she lay senseless on his breast.

For one awful moment the blackness returned upon him and swallowed him up, and he knew not what terrible thing had happened; but when a loud voice proclaimed the fact that the prince had ceased to live, a wild fury fell upon Paul, and he started to his feet to revenge that death by plunging his dagger into the breast of the haughty monarch as he stood there, calm and smiling, in his terrible wrath and power.

Had Paul attempted to carry out this wild act, a fateful murder would have been enacted in the tent that day; but even as he released himself from the clinging clasp of Anne's unconscious arms, there came to him the memory of those last words spoken by his beloved prince. The young bride must be his first care. She must be carried to safe sanctuary; that done, he would stand forth to revenge his lord's death. But the prince's charge must be fulfilled.

Lifting the unconscious form in his arms, he walked unchallenged from the tent. The deed now done sent a thrill of horror through the camp, and men looked into each other's eyes, and were ashamed that they had stood by to see it.

Not an attempt was made to oppose the passage of the faithful attendant, who carried in his arms the page boy, who had stood by his master to the last. Room was made for them to pass through the crowd; and staggering blindly along, Paul reached a spot where, to his astonishment and relief, his own servant was waiting for him with a horse ready caparisoned.

"To the church, to the church," he whispered as Paul mounted mechanically, holding his still unconscious burden in his arms.

And he made a mute sign of assent; for he knew that within the walls of the church he should find the wretched Margaret, who would have taken sanctuary there at first tidings of defeat.

Silently, and as in a dream, the horsemen passed along, and at last drew rein at the door of the little church, where stood

Evelyn Everett-Green

a priest with the Host in his hand, ready, if need be, to stand betwixt the helpless victims of the battle and their fierce pursuers.

He knew Paul's face, he recognized that of the inanimate form he carried in his arms, and he made way for him to pass with a mute sign of blessing.

Paul passed in. There beside the altar he saw the queen, bowed down by the magnitude of her woe, for she had just heard the first rumour of that terrible tragedy.

As he approached someone spoke to her, and she turned, rose, and came swiftly forward.

"Paul," she said, "Paul—tell me—is it true?"

Paul looked at her with dim eyes.

"I have brought you his wife," he said. "It was his last charge. Now I am going back. They have killed him; let them kill me, too."

He placed his helpless burden in the queen's arms, turned, and made a few uncertain steps, and then fell down helplessly. He had fulfilled his life's purpose in living for the prince; but it was not given to him to die uselessly for him, too.

CHAPTER 10

THE PRINCE AVENGED

Paul Stukely lived to see the foul crime that stained the victor's laurels on the field of Tewkesbury amply avenged upon the House of York in the days that quickly followed.

He himself was carried away by his faithful men-at-arms, who saw that their cause was finally lost; and when, many weeks later, the raging fever which held him in its grasp abated, and he knew once more the faces of those about him, and could ask what had befallen him, he found that he had been carried away to his own small manor, bestowed upon him by the great Earl of Warwick—which manor, perhaps from its very obscurity and his own, was left quietly in his hands; for its late owner had fallen upon the field of Tewkesbury, and no claim was ever made which disturbed Paul from peaceful possession.

When he recovered his senses it was to hear that not only the prince was dead, but his royal father also; that the queen, as Margaret was still called by him, had returned to France; and that the cause of the Red Rose was hopelessly extinguished. So Paul, with the hopefulness which is the prerogative of youth, recovered by degrees from the depression of spirit that the memory of the tragedy of Tewkesbury cast over him,

Evelyn Everett-Green

and learned by degrees to take a healthy interest in his little domain, which he ruled wisely and kindly, without meddling in public matters, or taking part in the burning questions of the day. To him Edward always was and always must be a cruel tyrant and usurper; but as none but princes of the House of York were left to claim the succession to the crown, there could be no possible object in any renewal of strife.

Paul, in his quiet west-country home, watched the progress of events, and saw in the tragedies which successively befell the scions of the House of York the vengeance of Heaven for the foul murder of the young Lancastrian prince.

The Duke of Clarence, who had been one of the first to strike him, fell a victim to the displeasure of the king, his brother, and was secretly put to death in the Tower. Although Edward himself died a natural death, it was said that vexation at the failure of some of his most treasured schemes for the advancement of his children cut him off in the flower of his age. And a darker fate befell his own young sons than he had inflicted upon the son of the rival monarch: for Edward of Lancaster had died a soldier's death, openly slain by the sword in the light of day; whilst the murderer's children were done to death between the stone walls of a prison, and for years their fate was shrouded in terrible mystery.

The next death in that ill-omened race was that of King Richard's own son, in the tenth year of his age. As Duke of Gloucester, he had stood by to see the death of young Edward, even if his hand had not been raised to strike him. He had then forced into reluctant wedlock with himself the betrothed bride of the murdered prince—the unhappy Lady Anne. He had murdered his brother's children to raise himself to the throne, and had committed many other crimes to maintain himself thereon; and his own son—another

Edward, Prince of Wales—was doomed to meet a sudden death, called by the chroniclers of the time "unhappy," as though some strange or painful circumstance attached to it, in the absence of both his parents: and lastly, the lonely monarch, wifeless and childless, was called upon to reap the fruits of the bitter hostility and distrust which his cruel and arbitrary rule had awakened in the breasts of his own nobles and of his subjects in general.

Paul Stukely, now a married man with children of his own growing up about him, watched with intense interest the course of public events; and when Henry of Richmond—a lineal descendant of Edward the Third by his son John of Gaunt—landed for the second time to head the insurrection against the bloody tyrant, Sir Paul Stukely and a gallant little following marched amongst the first to join his standard, and upon the bloody field of Bosworth, Paul felt that he saw revenged to the full the tragedy of Tewkesbury.

He was there, close beside Henry Tudor, when the last frantic charge of the wretched monarch in his despair was made, and when Richard, after unhorsing many amongst Henry's personal attendants in order to come to a hand-to-hand combat with his foe, witnessed the secession from his ranks of Sir William Stanley, and fell, crying "Treason, treason!" with his last breath. He who had obtained his crown by treachery, cruelty, and treason of the blackest kind, was destined to fall a victim to the treachery of others. As Paul saw the mangled corpse flung across a horse's back and carried ignominiously from the field, he felt that the God of heaven did indeed look down and visit with His vengeance those who had set at nought His laws, and that in the miserable death of this last son of the House of York the cause of the Red Rose was amply avenged.

A few years later, in the bright summertide, when the politic

Evelyn Everett-Green

rule of Henry the Seventh was causing the exhausted country to recover from the ravages of the long civil war, Sir Paul Stukely and his two sons, fine, handsome lads of ten and twelve years old, were making a little journey (as we should now call it, though it seemed a long one to the excited and delighted boys) from his pleasant manor near St. Albans through a part of the county of Essex.

Paul had prospered during these past years. The king had rewarded his early fealty by a grant of lands and a fine manor near to St. Albans, whither he had removed his wife and family, so as to be within easy reach of them at such times as he was summoned by the king to Westminster. The atmosphere of home was dearer to him than that of courts, and he was no longer away from his own house than his duty to his king obliged him to be. But he had been much engaged by public duties of late, and the holiday he had promised himself had been long in coming. It had been a promise of some standing to his two elder sons, Edward and Paul, that he would take them some day to visit the spots which he talked of when they climbed upon his knee after his day's work was done to beg for the story of "the little prince," as they still called him. Paul himself was eager again to visit those familiar haunts, and see if any of those who had befriended the homeless wanderer were living still, and would recognize the bronzed and prosperous knight of today.

And now they were entering a familiar tract; and the father told his boys to keep their eyes well open, for the village of Much Waltham could not be far off and every pathway in this part of the forest had been traversed by him and the prince in the days that had gone by.

"I hear the sound of hammering," cried the younger Paul in great excitement soon. "O father, we must be getting very near! It is like a smith's forge. I am sure it must be Will Ives or his father. Oh, do let us ride on quickly and see!"

The riders pressed onward through the widening forest path, and, sure enough, found themselves quickly in the little clearing which surrounded the village of Much Waltham. How well the elder Paul remembered it all! the village church, the smithy, and the low thatched cottages, the small gardens, now brighter than he had seen them in the dreary winter months; the whole place wearing an air of increased comfort and prosperity.

The flame within the forge burned cheerily, and revealed an active figure within, hard at work over some glowing metal, which emitted showers of brilliant sparks. Sir Paul rode forward and paused at the door with a smile of recognition on his face. The smith came forward to see if the traveller required any service of him, but was somewhat taken aback by the greeting he received.

"Well, worthy Will Ives, time has dealt more kindly with you than with me, I trow. You are scarce a whit changed from the day, seventeen years back come November, when I first stopped in sorry plight at this forge, with your pretty wife as my companion, to get your assistance as far as Figeon's Farm. Why, and here is Mistress Joan herself; and I warrant that that fine lad is the son of both of you.

"Good Even to you, fair mistress!—Last time we met we scarce thought that so many years would roll by before I should pay these parts a visit. But fortune's wheel has many strange turns, and I have been dwelling in regions far remote from here. But these lads of mine have given me no peace until I should bring them on a visit to Much Waltham and Figeon's Farm. I trust that I shall find all the dwellers there hale and hearty as of yore, and that death has passed this peaceful place by, whilst he has been so busy elsewhere."

　　　　　Evelyn Everett-Green

Great was the excitement of the place when it was realized by the inhabitants that this fine knight, who rode with half-a-dozen men-at-arms in his company, and two beautiful boys at his side, was none other than the Paul Stukely that the men and women of the place remembered, and the children spoke of as of the hero of some romance dear to their hearts. The news flew like wildfire through the village, and old and young came flocking out to see, till the knight was the centre of quite a little crowd, and the excited and delighted boys were hearing the familiar story again and again from the lips of these friendly strangers.

When at length the little cavalcade moved up the gentle slope toward Figeon's Farm, quite a large bodyguard accompanied it. Joan herself walked proudly beside the knight, who had given his horse in charge to his servant, and was on foot as he trod the familiar track; and she was listening with flushing and paling cheek to the tale of Tewkesbury, whilst the boys were asking questions of everybody in the little crowd, and eagerly pushing on ahead to get the first sight of the farm that had twice sheltered their father in the hour of his need.

The old people were living yet, though infirm and feeble, and more disposed to spend the day in the armchairs, beside the blazing fire in the inglenook, than to stir abroad or carry on any active occupation at home. Jack Devenish and his wife, Eva, managed the house and farm, and brought up their sturdy and numerous family so as to be a credit to the old name. It was Jack himself who came hurrying out to meet his guests—a rumour of their approach having gone on before—whilst his smiling wife stood in the door way to welcome in the bronzed knight, whom once she had rescued from such pitiful plight and from deadly danger.

What a welcome it was that they got from all at Figeon's

Farm! and how delightful to the boys to run all over the house—to see the room in which their father had slept, the window from which he had flung the robber who had come to carry away Mistress Joan, and the little sliding panel behind which the recess lay that had been so luckily emptied of its treasure before the search party came!

Then, on the next day, there was the Priory to visit, and Brother Lawrence to claim acquaintance with, and a long ride through the forest to be made to visit the cave at Black Notley, where Paul had once been dragged a prisoner, and had been so roughly handled by the robbers. The days were full of excitement and pleasure to the two lads, and scarcely less so to Paul himself, save for the faint flavour of melancholy which could not but at times assail him in recalling the episode of his romantic friendship with Edward, Prince of Wales.

And when they returned home at last to tell their adventures to wife and mother, they left behind them in Much Waltham many substantial proofs of the gratitude the Stukelys must ever feel for the protection accorded by its inhabitants in past days to the head of the house; and round the firesides in cottage and farm there was for many long years no more favourite story told by the old folks to the eager children than the tale of adventure, peril, and devotion in the days of the Wars of the Roses, which went by the name, in that place, of "The Story of Paul and the Prince."

Evelyn Everett-Green

Notes.

{1} Lichfield had the right in these days of calling itself a county.

Choose from Thousands of 1stWorldLibrary Classics By

A. M. Barnard
Ada Leverson
Adolphus William Ward
Aesop
Agatha Christie
Alexander Aaronsohn
Alexander Kielland
Alexandre Dumas
Alfred Gatty
Alfred Ollivant
Alice Duer Miller
Alice Turner Curtis
Alice Dunbar
Allen Chapman
Alleyne Ireland
Ambrose Bierce
Amelia E. Barr
Amory H. Bradford
Andrew Lang
Andrew McFarland Davis
Andy Adams
Angela Brazil
Anna Alice Chapin
Anna Sewell
Annie Besant
Annie Hamilton Donnell
Annie Payson Call
Annie Roe Carr
Annonaymous
Anton Chekhov
Archibald Lee Fletcher
Arnold Bennett
Arthur C. Benson
Arthur Conan Doyle
Arthur M. Winfield
Arthur Ransome
Arthur Schnitzler
Arthur Train
Atticus
B.H. Baden-Powell
B. M. Bower
B. C. Chatterjee
Baroness Emmuska Orczy
Baroness Orczy
Basil King
Bayard Taylor
Ben Macomber
Bertha Muzzy Bower
Bjornstjerne Bjornson

Booth Tarkington
Boyd Cable
Bram Stoker
C. Collodi
C. E. Orr
C. M. Ingleby
Carolyn Wells
Catherine Parr Traill
Charles A. Eastman
Charles Amory Beach
Charles Dickens
Charles Dudley Warner
Charles Farrar Browne
Charles Ives
Charles Kingsley
Charles Klein
Charles Hanson Towne
Charles Lathrop Pack
Charles Romyn Dake
Charles Whibley
Charles Willing Beale
Charlotte M. Braeme
Charlotte M. Yonge
Charlotte Perkins Stetson
Clair W. Hayes
Clarence Day Jr.
Clarence E. Mulford
Clemence Housman
Confucius
Coningsby Dawson
Cornelis DeWitt Wilcox
Cyril Burleigh
D. H. Lawrence
Daniel Defoe
David Garnett
Dinah Craik
Don Carlos Janes
Donald Keyhoe
Dorothy Kilner
Dougan Clark
Douglas Fairbanks
E. Nesbit
E. P. Roe
E. Phillips Oppenheim
E. S. Brooks
Earl Barnes
Edgar Rice Burroughs
Edith Van Dyne
Edith Wharton

Edward Everett Hale
Edward J. O'Biren
Edward S. Ellis
Edwin L. Arnold
Eleanor Atkins
Eleanor Hallowell Abbott
Eliot Gregory
Elizabeth Gaskell
Elizabeth McCracken
Elizabeth Von Arnim
Ellem Key
Emerson Hough
Emilie F. Carlen
Emily Bronte
Emily Dickinson
Enid Bagnold
Enilor Macartney Lane
Erasmus W. Jones
Ernie Howard Pie
Ethel May Dell
Ethel Turner
Ethel Watts Mumford
Eugene Sue
Eugenie Foa
Eugene Wood
Eustace Hale Ball
Evelyn Everett-green
Everard Cotes
F. H. Cheley
F. J. Cross
F. Marion Crawford
Fannie E. Newberry
Federick Austin Ogg
Ferdinand Ossendowski
Fergus Hume
Florence A. Kilpatrick
Fremont B. Deering
Francis Bacon
Francis Darwin
Frances Hodgson Burnett
Frances Parkinson Keyes
Frank Gee Patchin
Frank Harris
Frank Jewett Mather
Frank L. Packard
Frank V. Webster
Frederic Stewart Isham
Frederick Trevor Hill
Frederick Winslow Taylor

Friedrich Kerst	Hayden Carruth	James Branch Cabell
Friedrich Nietzsche	Helent Hunt Jackson	James DeMille
Fyodor Dostoyevsky	Helen Nicolay	James Joyce
G.A. Henty	Hendrik Conscience	James Lane Allen
G.K. Chesterton	Hendy David Thoreau	James Lane Allen
Gabrielle E. Jackson	Henri Barbusse	James Oliver Curwood
Garrett P. Serviss	Henrik Ibsen	James Oppenheim
Gaston Leroux	Henry Adams	James Otis
George A. Warren	Henry Ford	James R. Driscoll
George Ade	Henry Frost	Jane Abbott
Geroge Bernard Shaw	Henry James	Jane Austen
George Cary Eggleston	Henry Jones Ford	Jane L. Stewart
George Durston	Henry Seton Merriman	Janet Aldridge
George Ebers	Henry W Longfellow	Jens Peter Jacobsen
George Eliot	Herbert A. Giles	Jerome K. Jerome
George Gissing	Herbert Carter	Jessie Graham Flower
George MacDonald	Herbert N. Casson	John Buchan
George Meredith	Herman Hesse	John Burroughs
George Orwell	Hildegard G. Frey	John Cournos
George Sylvester Viereck	Homer	John F. Kennedy
George Tucker	Honore De Balzac	John Gay
George W. Cable	Horace B. Day	John Glasworthy
George Wharton James	Horace Walpole	John Habberton
Gertrude Atherton	Horatio Alger Jr.	John Joy Bell
Gordon Casserly	Howard Pyle	John Kendrick Bangs
Grace E. King	Howard R. Garis	John Milton
Grace Gallatin	Hugh Lofting	John Philip Sousa
Grace Greenwood	Hugh Walpole	John Taintor Foote
Grant Allen	Humphry Ward	Jonas Lauritz Idemil Lie
Guillermo A. Sherwell	Ian Maclaren	Jonathan Swift
Gulielma Zollinger	Inez Haynes Gillmore	Joseph A. Altsheler
Gustav Flaubert	Irving Bacheller	Joseph Carey
H. A. Cody	Isabel Cecilia Williams	Joseph Conrad
H. B. Irving	Isabel Hornibrook	Joseph E. Badger Jr
H.C. Bailey	Israel Abrahams	Joseph Hergesheimer
H. G. Wells	Ivan Turgenev	Joseph Jacobs
H. H. Munro	J.G.Austin	Jules Vernes
H. Irving Hancock	J. Henri Fabre	Julian Hawthrone
H. R. Naylor	J. M. Barrie	Julie A Lippmann
H. Rider Haggard	J. M. Walsh	Justin Huntly McCarthy
H. W. C. Davis	J. Macdonald Oxley	Kakuzo Okakura
Haldeman Julius	J. R. Miller	Karle Wilson Baker
Hall Caine	J. S. Fletcher	Kate Chopin
Hamilton Wright Mabie	J. S. Knowles	Kenneth Grahame
Hans Christian Andersen	J. Storer Clouston	Kenneth McGaffey
Harold Avery	J. W. Duffield	Kate Langley Bosher
Harold McGrath	Jack London	Kate Langley Bosher
Harriet Beecher Stowe	Jacob Abbott	Katherine Cecil Thurston
Harry Castlemon	James Allen	Katherine Stokes
Harry Coghill	James Andrews	L. A. Abbot
Harry Houidini	James Baldwin	L. T. Meade

L. Frank Baum
Latta Griswold
Laura Dent Crane
Laura Lee Hope
Laurence Housman
Lawrence Beasley
Leo Tolstoy
Leonid Andreyev
Lewis Carroll
Lewis Sperry Chafer
Lilian Bell
Lloyd Osbourne
Louis Hughes
Louis Joseph Vance
Louis Tracy
Louisa May Alcott
Lucy Fitch Perkins
Lucy Maud Montgomery
Luther Benson
Lydia Miller Middleton
Lyndon Orr
M. Corvus
M. H. Adams
Margaret E. Sangster
Margret Howth
Margaret Vandercook
Margaret W. Hungerford
Margret Penrose
Maria Edgeworth
Maria Thompson Daviess
Mariano Azuela
Marion Polk Angellotti
Mark Overton
Mark Twain
Mary Austin
Mary Catherine Crowley
Mary Cole
Mary Hastings Bradley
Mary Roberts Rinehart
Mary Rowlandson
M. Wollstonecraft Shelley
Maud Lindsay
Max Beerbohm
Myra Kelly
Nathaniel Hawthrone
Nicolo Machiavelli
O. F. Walton
Oscar Wilde

Owen Johnson
P.G. Wodehouse
Paul and Mabel Thorne
Paul G. Tomlinson
Paul Severing
Percy Brebner
Percy Keese Fitzhugh
Peter B. Kyne
Plato
Quincy Allen
R. Derby Holmes
R. L. Stevenson
R. S. Ball
Rabindranath Tagore
Rahul Alvares
Ralph Bonehill
Ralph Henry Barbour
Ralph Victor
Ralph Waldo Emmerson
Rene Descartes
Ray Cummings
Rex Beach
Rex E. Beach
Richard Harding Davis
Richard Jefferies
Richard Le Gallienne
Robert Barr
Robert Frost
Robert Gordon Anderson
Robert L. Drake
Robert Lansing
Robert Lynd
Robert Michael Ballantyne
Robert W. Chambers
Rosa Nouchette Carey
Rudyard Kipling
Saint Augustine
Samuel B. Allison
Samuel Hopkins Adams
Sarah Bernhardt
Sarah C. Hallowell
Selma Lagerlof
Sherwood Anderson
Sigmund Freud
Standish O'Grady
Stanley Weyman
Stella Benson
Stella M. Francis

Stephen Crane
Stewart Edward White
Stijn Streuvels
Swami Abhedananda
Swami Parmananda
T. S. Ackland
T. S. Arthur
The Princess Der Ling
Thomas A. Janvier
Thomas A Kempis
Thomas Anderton
Thomas Bailey Aldrich
Thomas Bulfinch
Thomas De Quincey
Thomas Dixon
Thomas H. Huxley
Thomas Hardy
Thomas More
Thornton W. Burgess
U. S. Grant
Upton Sinclair
Valentine Williams
Various Authors
Vaughan Kester
Victor Appleton
Victor G. Durham
Victoria Cross
Virginia Woolf
Wadsworth Camp
Walter Camp
Walter Scott
Washington Irving
Wilbur Lawton
Wilkie Collins
Willa Cather
Willard F. Baker
William Dean Howells
William le Queux
W. Makepeace Thackeray
William W. Walter
William Shakespeare
Winston Churchill
Yei Theodora Ozaki
Yogi Ramacharaka
Young E. Allison
Zane Grey